Talk to Me God Devotionals

100 Modern Stories to Brighten Each Day, Deposit Wisdom and Inspire Success

Dr. Timothy Jackson Jr.

Ordering Information:

Orders by U.S. trade bookstores and wholesalers. Quantity sales. Special discounts are available on quantity purchases by corporations, associations, and others. For details, contact the publisher at the following email address: PastorTimothyJacksonJr@gmail.com

Connect with Dr. Timothy Jackson:

Instagram: https://www.instagram.com/iamtimjackson/
Facebook: https://www.facebook.com/PastorTimothyJacksonJr

3750 Hacks Cross Road
Ste. 102-363
Memphis, TN 38125
PastorTimothyJacksonJr@gmail.com
(901) 779-4229

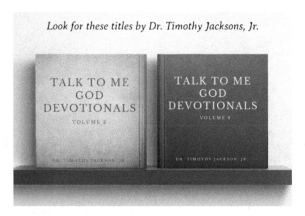

Look for these titles by Dr. Timothy Jacksons, Jr.

ISBN: 978-0-578-79191-3

Dedication

This book is dedicated to my wonderful wife, Ashiqua, who has been nothing short of supportive since the very beginning. Thank you for not allowing fear and insecurity to cause me not to bring this to fruition. What a blessing you have been and continue to be.

This book is also dedicated to my wonderful children, Ava, Timothy III, and Avery. The formation of this book began before any of you were born, but the finale of the book is because of you. Not only have you been great fodder for the devotionals, but I pray this will encourage you to pursue the greatness that is in each of you. My hope is one day you will be as proud to have me as your father as I am to be your father. Daddy loves you more than words can ever express!

This project is also dedicated to my parents Timothy Jackson, Sr. and my late mother, Mae Ree Jackson, who believed in me more than I believed in myself. Over the years, there have been many days I have longed to have you here and this book is no exception. I can only imagine how excited you would be in celebrating this moment. One thing is for certain, I carried you with me every step of the way. I love you and miss you more than these few words can convey.

To the great members of Hope Fellowship Church Memphis, you are simply the best church a pastor could ask or *hope* for. One of my greatest joys in life is serving as your pastor. I look forward to our future as Pastor and people.

Table of Contents

Introduction

Simplicity is life. Think about the truth of this for a minute. Let your mind wander back to the last time you laughed with a friend, lingered over coffee, played boardgames with the family or any of the countless moments nestled between the "big" moments. You're already familiar with those BIG moments like weddings, funerals, graduations and baptisms. However, when you think about it, the majority of our lived experiences happen on either side of events such as these. Let's unpack the significance of this.

Life's solutions are revealed in the simple moments. At first look, maybe someone else might not consider your moments remarkable at all. But I discovered a secret. Important life lessons are scattered throughout my daily routines and experiences. We can see examples of this in the many parables written throughout the Bible.

Many have received deep revelation after reading parables about:

- People working in a field
- Wine running out
- A man going on a business trip
- Seeds
- A lost sheep
- Women standing in a line
- A wayward son
- Hidden treasures
- A fancy dinner
- A tree
- A mean judge … and more!

You have to admit that none of these biblical principles are presented in an overly deep way, yet they somehow have impact. There's a reason God's word is written like this! You deserve to model God's simple method as you seek Him throughout your own life. In this book, I'll show you how God drops the most transformative wisdom in the situations you face every day. The *Talk to Me God* series is filled with 100 modern parables from my own life that you can apply to whatever situation you're facing. As you read through each story, and seek God, you'll begin to hear Him pointing out simple solutions to complex problems, just as he did for me! Here is just a sample of what you'll discover while you read this and other books in the *Talk to Me God* series:

If you've ever felt lost, or like the future is bleak ... God gave me the deepest revelation and filled my heart with hope while I sat feeling frustrated at my desk one day.

If you've ever wondered how to let God do His thing ... God showed me how to literally "let go and let God" while cutting grass with my father.

If you've ever struggled with impatience ... God gave me the answer as I tried to encourage my daughter who was crying about her dress that didn't fit any longer.

If you've ever wondered about your life's calling ... Directions from God regarding this time-tested question came in the form of an anonymous phone call.

If you ever felt broken ... I learned a valuable life lesson and much encouragement while coloring with my children.

I invite you to spend the next 100 days with me as you learn new ways to connect with God. At the back of this devotional, I've included some pages where you can take notes and chart your journey. As you expose yourself to modern stories of the many ways God has heard *me* when I pray ... may it help you to know that when *you* cry out in frustration or confusion, "Talk to me, God!" He certainly hears you and responds in the most unexpected ways.

I'll see you on the inside ...

God Uses Broken Pieces

"But we have this treasure in jars of clay to show that this all-surpassing power is from God and not from us."

— *II Corinthians 4:7 (NIV)*

When my oldest daughter was a toddler, we spent time with one another playing chalk in front of our house. We were on the sidewalk drawing pictures of various things, and at some point she broke her piece of chalk. When she broke her piece of chalk, she handed it to me and said, "Daddy, you use this." I said, "Ava, I didn't break the chalk, you broke your chalk, why are you handing it to me?" As if I did not say anything, she said again, "Daddy, you use this." Again, I said, "But, Ava, I did not break your chalk, you broke it, now you want me to use your broken piece of chalk." She again ignored me and said, "Daddy, you use it." My daughter was confident her father could use her broken piece. Needless to say, I relented and began drawing pictures with the broken piece of chalk my daughter handed to me.

In this moment, I discovered this is how God operates with us, His children. In life we can find ourselves holding on to broken pieces: broken relationships, broken marriages, broken friendships, broken self-esteem, etc. Nevertheless, whatever broken pieces that exist in our lives, if we hand them to the Father, we will soon discover God can draw beautiful pictures with our broken pieces. No matter what is broken in your life, no matter the circumstance or situation that has broken or fractured you, if you hand it to the Father, your God can use all of your broken pieces. God will use the broken pieces to draw the picture He has in mind for your life.

A Better Fit

"Therefore, since we are surrounded by such a great cloud of witnesses, let us throw off everything that hinders and the sin that so easily entangles. And let us run with perseverance the race marked out for us."

— *Hebrews 12:1 (NIV)*

"Therefore, if anyone is in Christ, the new creation has come: The old has gone, the new is here!"

— *II Corinthians 5:17 (NIV)*

One Sunday morning, I told my youngest daughter to find something to wear to church. She went to her room and brought a dress back to me for approval. I looked at the dress and determined the dress was too small for her. I instructed her to go to her closet and find something else to wear. To my dismay, she burst into tears. When I inquired about her crying, with a tear-filled voice, she said, "Because I want to wear the dress." I said, "Avery, the dress is too small for you, you need to put it in the giveaway box with the other things you have outgrown. I did not say anything was wrong with the dress, the dress is just too small for where you are." As she continued to cry, I was dually frustrated and disappointed because my daughter was crying about something she had outgrown. As her father, I was frustrated because I had purchased and placed new clothes in her closet that were purposed solely for her, but she overlooked them. Over the course of her life, I have regularly purchased the clothes she needs but also clothes she likes. Nevertheless, my dear daughter was grieving because her growth caused something to no longer fit her.

My frustration/disappointment did not last long as I considered the fact that many people are just like my daughter. God has grown you in various ways to where you have outgrown things and some people around you. God is dually frustrated and disappointed because sometimes you become attached to where you are, and/or the past, that you would rather forfeit the new and remain attached to the old. God has provided some new things in the closet of life that are awaiting you to pick them up: new opportunities, new people, and new things. This is the season to say goodbye to the people and things that no longer fit and embrace the new that God has in store for you.

Just Get Through

"Even though I walk through the darkest valley ... "

— *Psalm 23:4 (NIV)*

My family and I attended a birthday party at some friend's house for one of their children. The parents of the birthday boy elected to get a bouncy house for the kids to enjoy. It rained earlier in the day so the ground was a little muddy, so the kids had to walk through a little mud in order to get to the bouncy house. While most of the kids did not mind going through the mud, that was not the case of one little girl. One little girl was excited as she took off her shoes and made her trek to the bouncy house. Unexpectedly, she reached a muddy point and when she stepped in the mud, she stopped and began to cry because she was not accustomed to being in the mud. The mud was uncomfortable to her, so the mud stopped her from reaching where she wanted to go.

In reality, this is a depiction of our lives. Sometimes life lands us in some uncomfortable and painful places. Rather than continuing to move forward because the destination is just ahead, we get stuck and begin to cry. Not only do we begin to cry, we also murmur and complain, and allow our feelings to impede our progress. Though life gets difficult sometimes and you may even get emotional, do not allow your emotions to keep you from being in motion. The moment, the difficulty, the trial, or the tribulation is only temporary. God is with you, just get through. The destination is just ahead.

Wait

"But those who hope in the Lord will renew their strength; they will soar on wings like eagles..."

- Isaiah 40:31 (NIV)

As a child, I would try and cut the grass with my Dad. The lawnmower was way too big for me, but I was determined to help my dad out. I vividly recall one day while cutting the grass, he decided to take a break and go back in the house. I didn't feel like taking a break, so when he went in the house, I began to cut the grass myself. I must say that didn't work out too well. When I cut it, the lines were crooked, and I missed spots throughout the yard, among other things, to my Dad's dismay. Ultimately, my Dad really didn't need my help. I messed up the yard because I was trying to operate a mower that was too big for me. My Dad had experience and it was more than enough to handle the yard without me. In that moment, I quickly figured out that I needed to get out of the way and let my Dad do what he knew how to do.

One of the worst things we can do is to get in God's way. God is working in our lives, but oftentimes we step in to help Him out. There are times in our lives when it seems like God has gone in the house and forgotten about our situation. When He is not moving in accordance with our timing, we take matters into our own hands, only to end up messing things up. We go when God says stop. We stop when God says go. We step in when God says step out. You get the picture. As tempting as it may be, you cannot give in to the temptation to help God out when things are not happening as quickly as you would like. Someone once said, "To us, waiting is wasting, but to God, waiting is working." The reality is that what you face is too big for you to handle. Stepping in will only mess up what God is trying to do in your life, resulting in crooked situations and missed opportunities. Whatever you are facing, get out of the way and let Dad do what He wants to do, when He wants to do it, and how He wants to get it done.

Blank Pages

"Trust in the Lord with all your heart and lean not on your own understanding; in all your ways submit to him, and he will make your paths straight."

— *Proverbs 3:5-6 (NIV)*

In my corporate job, a significant amount of my time is spent submitting applications and reports to various agencies throughout the country. I vividly recall the frustration I experienced my first time completing an application. The application was extremely long and tedious that included a number of legal terms I had never heard before. I plodded through, then I got to what I thought was the end because I had reached a blank page. Thinking I was done, I threw my hands up in relief because it was over, it was finished, I was done.

To my chagrin, I looked at the bottom of the page and it said, "This page is intentionally left blank." I turned the page only to find another section of the application that needed to be completed. At this point, I wanted to speak in familiar tongues as I sat at my desk wondering why someone would intentionally insert a blank page in the middle of the application packet. I took the packet into my manager and said, "Why do they put blank pages in this thing, that makes no sense?" She looked at me and said, "Tim, the blank pages are there to separate the sections and to let you know there is more to come."

There are times in life when the future looks blank, uncertain, or maybe even dismal or dead. During these times, you have no idea what is next. You are unsure what the next move is, unsure of what you should do, where you should go, if you should go, what's going to happen... the list goes on. You consistently and fervently petition God in prayer, yet He seems unresponsive and uninterested in your passionate pleas or requests. You need to know that sometimes God intentionally places blank pages in your life to separate your seasons and to let you know more is coming. The next phase/season is on the horizon. Note where you are and where you have been because your story has not concluded; God has more in store for you. When you find yourself in this place, "Trust in the Lord with all thine heart; and lean not unto thine own understanding. In all thy ways acknowledge him, and He shall direct thy paths." Trust in God's timing, rely on His promises, wait for His answers, and relax in His Presence because there is more to come. These trials are just blank pages.

Walk Blindfolded

"For we live by faith, not by sight. "

—II Corinthians 5:7 (NIV)

"Trust in the Lord with all your heart and lean not on your own understanding; "

- Proverbs 3:5 (NIV)

Several years ago, I participated in a team building exercise, where a group of us were taken to a wooded area, blindfolded, and instructed to walk in no particular direction. We were in an unfamiliar place, nervous and unable to see where we were going. However, there was a person standing nearby without a blindfold who instructed us about where to go, where not to go, what to do and what not to do. While we could not see where we were going, he could. The intention of the exercise was to teach us to trust the voice of the person speaking because he could see what we were unable to see.

There are times where you feel you're in the woods of life ... where life is uncomfortable, unfamiliar, and seems to have no particular direction. You feel as if you are walking through life blindfolded because you cannot see clearly or understand the why of where you are in life. It is paramount that you understand that sometimes God allows you to experience unfamiliar or uncomfortable situations where no clear direction or purpose can be identified. It is then that you have to depend on the voice of God, the One without a blindfold. Maybe you have found yourself in a wooded area of life, you are nervous and have no idea of how (or if) you will navigate through it. Certainly, it can become challenging to trust in the Lord when you lack understanding. Nevertheless, it is in this season that you must walk blindfolded by leaning on, and trusting God who sees what we cannot.

It's Not All About You

"Give thanks to the LORD, for he is good; his love endures forever. Let the redeemed of the LORD tell their story — those he redeemed from the hand of the foe ..."

— Psalm 107:1-2 (NIV)

"Though you have made me see troubles, many and bitter, you will restore my life again; from the depths of the earth you will again bring me up. You will increase my honor and comfort me once again."

— Psalm 71:20-21 (NIV)

At the conclusion of a three-week ACT workshop, as the youth pastor, I decided to give a prize to the student who attended every session and had the lowest ACT score. I simply wanted to acknowledge the student's obvious quest for improvement. The young lady that fit the bill was hurt and embarrassed about her ACT score and refused to tell me what it was. However, she told an instructor who then shared her score with me. When I was told what the score was, amazingly it was the EXACT score I made when I took the test the first time! For the inquiring minds, my score was an incredible 15. Reminded of the hurt and embarrassment I had experienced, I took the opportunity to encourage the young lady from the position of a person who scored a 15. What fortified my influence was the fact that I was then a college graduate working in my field and maintaining a 3.8 GPA as a graduate student. To see the young lady's face light up with hope still warms my heart. Little did I know that what

I experienced in high school would pave the way for me to encourage someone else.

All of us can attest to the fact that life can dish out some painful and sometimes embarrassing moments. There are moments when we wonder or even cry out, "God, why me?" because we do not understand why we have to experience such pain and difficulty. When we begin to ask why, we must understand that God does not put heavy loads or experiences on weak shoulders. In addition, what we may discover weeks, months, or even years later, is that what we experienced was not solely for us, but for someone else who needs to hear from us out of our experience. Not only is experience the best teacher, but experience is the best testimony. Sharing from what you know is much more powerful than sharing from what you heard/read. There are some people who are experiencing some really challenging times right now and feel *picked on* when God has strategically *picked out* those whom He will use to bless the life of someone else. This too will pass and when it does pass, we must remember to pass the testimony on to someone else that is passing through. Let the redeemed of the Lord, say so!

It's Your Turn

"Yet the Lord longs to be gracious to you; therefore he will rise up to show you compassion. For the Lord is a God of justice. Blessed are all who wait for him!"

— *Isaiah 30:18 (NIV)*

As I drove the city streets, I came to a traffic light where I wanted to make a left turn. At the moment, it seemed as if everyone else in the city was trying to make the same turn. After a few series of lights, I gradually approached the light for my turn, but I was becoming impatient. I was confident I would eventually reach the light, but in my mind, it was taking too long for me to get there. When I finally reached the front of the line of the cars, I was finally given a green arrow, the official signal that I had the right away and all traffic had to stop until I passed through the light. Interestingly, after I made my turn, I did not think about the waiting, I was just glad my turn came.

There are times when you can pray for certain things to happen in your life and it seems as if you are watching everyone else be blessed, but the same blessings seem to evade you. At times, you literally witness the answering of your prayers in the lives of other people. The question that brews in the mind when this occurs is, "When will my turn come? You must know that in order to get your turn (blessing), it is vital that you stay in line. You must stay in God's will. When you become fatigued with waiting in line, know that you are slowly but surely approaching your turn. Of course, it can become exasperating to watch others *turn*, but be encouraged that your turn will come. In the meantime, trust God in this time, until it is your turn. God is going to give YOU the green arrow, the blessing that is only for you. When God releases it, do not reflect on the wait, but relish in the fact that it's your turn.

Can God Trust You With More?

"His master replied, 'Well done, good and faithful servant! You have been faithful with a few things; I will put you in charge of many things ..."

— *Matthew 25:21 (NIV)*

Gold jewelry was extremely popular in the 80s and 90s. As a teenager, I persistently begged my mother for a 14K gold rope necklace. I pleaded with her for months on end to buy me a *sizable* chain. Though it was expensive, she finally agreed to buy the necklace. She purchased the chain, but it was much smaller than the chain I desired. Like many teenagers, I did not hesitate to question her decision to buy me the smaller chain. She explained to me that she bought a small necklace so she could determine how I would treat the sizeable necklace I desired. The smaller necklace was nice, but my mother was willing to give me a better one on the condition that I take care of the one I had. She said, "If you take good care of the small necklace, I will be convinced you will take care of a better necklace." For the next several months, I cleaned and maintained the small necklace because I knew my mother would give me bigger and better.

Have you ever asked God for bigger and better? Maybe you have a desire for a bigger home, newer car, better clothes, better job, a bigger church, a larger ministry/career goal or something else. Maybe you have been petitioning God for months (maybe even years) and wonder why God has not granted your request(s). The ultimate question is, *can God trust you with more?* Whatever you are praying for, be certain to be a good steward of what you have. If you are a good steward of the small things, God just may give you bigger and better because of your faithfulness.

Losing to Win

"And we know that all things God works for the good of those who love him, who have been called according to his purpose."

— *Romans 8:28 (NIV)*

"Being confident of this, that he who began a good work in you will carry it on to completion until the day of Christ Jesus."

— *Philippians 1:6 (NIV)*

When my youngest daughter learned to write, she wanted to write as frequently as she could. I began keeping a pen and notebook in my car so she can write whenever she desired. One morning, she was in the backseat writing her letters, holding them up for me to see in the rearview mirror. She wrote the letter *L,* but when she flipped it up, her *L* morphed into the number *7.* She held it up and said, "Daddy, look at my *L.*" I said, "Avery, you wrote an *L,* but when you flip it, your *L* turns into a *7.*" She didn't understand how her *L* became a *7.* She was doing it correctly, but her father's view in the mirror saw a *7* and not an *L.*

The number 7 is a beloved number for most Christians because it denotes completion. The Christian life is filled with many ups, downs, highs, lows, mountains and valleys. Sometimes we win and sometimes we lose. When we lose, we often refer to the loss as an *L.* However, God has an amazing way of flipping our *L*'s into completions. In every loss, God divinely weaves our *L*'s for our good. No matter what losses you have experienced or are experiencing, you cannot afford to get trapped in the L. You must keep moving forward because one day you will look in the rearview mirror of your life and conclude that God completed every L you experienced. There is no L that God cannot flip, and when He flips it, completion happens at the same time.

God Makes the Difference

"Cast all your anxiety on him because he cares for you. Be alert and of sober mind. Your enemy the devil prowls around like a roaring lion looking for someone to devour."

— I Peter 5:7-8 (NIV)

One day I was at Jiffy Lube getting the oil changed on my vehicle. Having some spare time, I decided to wait while they worked on my car. They finished the work and I was beckoned to the counter to pay. I walked up to the counter and the guy told me the cost of the oil change. I reached into my pocket and began to count my money, and discovered I was short some change. Because I was short, I began to apologize to the cashier for being unable to remit the payment they deserved. In the midst of my being short, a man sitting nearby reached around me, put the money on the counter, and said "I'll make up the difference."

There are times in life when we are short. Most can relate to being short on money, but oftentimes we are short in other areas. Joy is short, peace is short, patience is short, health is short, resume is short, credit is short, and multitude of other things. In whatever areas of your life that you are short, there is a God who stands behind you. Despite how it seems, God is not blind to our tears, deaf to our prayers, or silent to our pains. There is One who makes up the difference when we come up short. God sees, God hears, and God will deliver.

The saints of old would sing it like this, *"Be not dismayed whatever betide, God will take care of you! Beneath His wings of love abide, God will take care of you! God will take care of you, through every day, o'er all the way; He will take care of you; God will take care of you!"* God makes the difference!

19

Covered Under Warranty

"If we claim to be without sin, we deceive ourselves and the truth is not in us. If we confess our sins, he is faithful and just and will forgive us our sins and purify us from ALL unrighteousness."

— *I John 1:8-9 (NIV)*

When I purchased my first car, I also purchased a bumper-to-bumper warranty. The warranty covered everything on the car and anything that could go wrong with it. If anything went wrong with the car, I could simply take the car to the dealership, pay a deductible and the car would be fixed. Some people in my realm felt the purchase of a warranty was a waste of money. However, I and others felt it was a worthy idea because there was always a chance something could go wrong. Therefore, the bumper to bumper warranty protected me just in case the car needed repair.

When you give your life to Christ, Jesus wipes away all sins. To give your life to Christ is to exchange your life for a life in Christ. At the close of the transaction of trading the old life for a new life in Christ, believers are provided a spiritual bumper to bumper warranty that literally covers ALL sins - past, present, and future. The truth is there is always a chance you could do something wrong (sin) - and we do! When you realize the need for spiritual repair, you remit a deductible of confession and repentance, and receive the repair and restoration of God's forgiveness. You are covered under God's warranty!

Stay In the Batter's Box

"In the land of Uz there lived a man whose name was Job. This man was blameless and upright; he feared God and shunned evil...Then the LORD said to Satan, 'Have you considered my servant Job? There is no one on earth like him; he is blameless and upright, a man who fears God and shuns evil.'"

—Job 1:1-8 (NIV)

In the game of baseball, there are white lines that outline the batter's boxes near home plate. There is a batter's box for everyone – both left-handed and right-handed hitters. When the batter steps into the batter's box, it serves as a signal to the pitcher to throw pitches with the sole goal of striking the batter out. The pitcher has various pitches in his repertoire in order to strike batters out — curve ball, fast ball, slider, etc. However, he only pitches to those who have both feet in the batter's box. The pitcher will not pitch to someone who is completely outside the batter's box or one who only has one foot in. Both feet must be in the batter's box for the pitcher to pitch.

Have you ever noticed that when you step into the will of God that is when the enemy unleashes his attack? When we are in God's will, we essentially step into His batter's box. It serves as a signal to the enemy to begin to commence throwing pitches in an attempt to get you off course. Of course, the enemy has various pitches he throws, but you must remain in the batter's box. The enemy only pitches to those who pose a threat. He will not pitch to those who are out of God's will; there is no reason to because they lack a formidable threat.

The enemy also does not pitch to those who are on both sides of the fence (lukewarm Christians). Nevertheless, the enemy only pitches to those who have both feet in the batter's box. You may be wondering why you are being attacked in so many areas of your life. Your marriage is under attack. Your children are under attack. You are under attack mentally and physically. The attacks you are experiencing may be an indication that you are in the batter's box. Like Job, you may feel picked on, but you may be picked out. Sometimes this game of life gets difficult and the devil throws voluminous pitches. Through it all, be encouraged to stand fast and stay in the batter's box. That is His will for your life.

Depend on God

"But he said to me, 'My grace is sufficient for you, for my power is made perfect in weakness.' Therefore, I will boast all the more gladly about my weaknesses, so that Christ's power may rest on me."

— *2 Corinthians 12:9 (NIV)*

In my free time in college, I spent a significant amount of time playing the card game, Spades. In Spades, there are four people consisting of two teams. The goal of the game is to see who can win the most *books.* One day while playing the game, the cards were dealt, and I was very dissatisfied with my hand. When looked at my hand, I said to myself, *"There is no way I will win with this."* I thought about throwing it in and giving up, but I decided to play it out and see what happens — even though I thought winning was impossible. As I played what I considered to be a bad hand, I discovered my partner was winning all the books. As the game continued, I simply began to depend on my partner rather than on my own hand to win the game. At the conclusion of the game, I was a winner because I depended on my partner to do what I could not.

In the game of life, sometimes you feel that you have been dealt a bad hand. The situation, circumstance, roll book, or financial situation looks too bleak to accomplish what you have been praying for. When you look at your position and what you are striving for, you become dissatisfied and conclude, *"There is no way I can win with this hand."* You think about throwing it in and giving up. When you look at where you are, you want to quit, you want to resign, you want to leave, and throw in the towel. Accept the challenge to play it out and see what happens — despite feeling that winning is impossible. As you continue to move forward with what you believe to be a bad hand, you will discover that your Partner (God) can/will win all the *books* you need to win what you are seeking God for. It is vital that you depend wholly on His hand and what He can do, rather than on what you can do. In the end, you will be a winner because you depended on your Partner to do what you could not.

Your Water Has Broken

"As has just been said: 'Today, if you hear his voice, do not harden your hearts as you did in the rebellion.'"

— *Hebrews 3:15 (NIV)*

Prior to having my own children, I was amazed by the miracle of childbirth while watching a show about labor and delivery. This particular show featured a woman whose water broke in her sixth month of pregnancy. When her water broke, she was swiftly transported to the hospital for immediate childbirth. Despite the fact that she was giving birth three months early, her situation forced her to do so. Certainly, early birth was not her preference because both her mind and her biological clock suggested the time had not yet come. When the doctors advised her to deliver the baby despite the earliness of the birth, she agreed because she wanted to do what was best for the child in her womb.

What about you? Have you been thinking about changing your career, starting a ministry, writing a book, going back to school, or launching a business? Is there something that you cannot seem to shake? Is there something you have strongly considered? Is there something you feel a heavy push to do? Could it be that you have been in labor for quite some time now - thinking, saving money, researching, training, etc. You have been going through years of virtual *Lamaze* trying to prepare for the birth. You may feel it is not time, but God may be saying to you, "Your water has broken, and NOW is your time to give birth to what is in you." In your mind, right now would be too soon, but after your water has broken, you need to step out of your comfort zone and know God is ready to birth what He has placed in your womb.

Tired of Waiting

"So is my word that goes out from my mouth: It will not return to me empty, but will accomplish what I desire and achieve the purpose for which I sent it."

— *Isaiah 55:11 (NIV)*

A friend of mine was helping his son with a cooking project he was instructed to do for a class. He and his son carefully read the directions and began to prepare the dish. Two hours passed and the dish did not exhibit the characteristics the directions advised to expect. At that point, a decision had to be made — start over or allow the dish to sit for a while longer than what the directions stated. Nevertheless, despite what it looked like; quitting was not an option. After allowing the dish to sit a while longer, the dish began to exhibit the characteristics described in the directions and they were able to complete the project. This was a subtle reminder that things sometimes do not happen in the time period that we expect them to.

Have you ever found yourself frustrated about the lack of results in your life? You have put forth all of your effort, you have dotted every "i" and crossed every "t." Despite your tremendous efforts, you see virtually no progress. This is especially frustrating when you are doing something you sense God has instructed you to do. Frustration can arise when you are perpetually the bridesmaid/groomsman, but it seems you are not even close to being a bride/groom. Frustration can arise when you offer a great product or service, but customers are slim to none. Frustration can arise when you have a stellar work performance, but promotion evades you and lands on someone who is less qualified.

This kind of frustration can exist in business, academia, relationships, marriage, church, etc. Despite our frustrations, we must hold on to the promise God made in His Word, "It SHALL accomplish the purpose for which I sent it." God's timing is different from our timing. Be encouraged that God has not forgotten His promises for He will do what He said He would do — in HIS time. One writer summarizes it perfectly, "No matter how long it takes, when God is at work, it is always worth the wait."

Drop It in the Mailbox

"... Let us throw off everything that hinders and the sin that so easily entangles. And let us run with perseverance the race marked out for us."

— Hebrews 12:1 (NIV)

One afternoon, I took notice of mail on my counter waiting to be sent out. Truthfully, the mail should have been sent some time ago. It had been sitting on the counter for weeks; to my dismay the mail would not send itself. Nevertheless, it was up to me to stamp it and place it in the mailbox. Placing stamps on the mail certainly indicated my desire to have it sent out, but that was not enough. However, placing it in the mailbox and raising the flag served as a signal to the mail carrier that there were some things at my home that needed to be sent. I was therefore giving him or her permission to pick it up and send it to its destination. Amusingly, when the mail carrier picked up the mail, he also dropped off some pieces that would require me to pay out some money!

Everyone faces difficulties, challenges, and issues in life. A lot of us (probably all of us) have issues in our lives that need to be sent out. The same issues have been sitting on the countertops of our hearts and minds a considerable amount of time. We undoubtedly know they need to be sent out of our lives, yet the same issues remain. Maybe our issues comprise of habits, unforgiveness, past hurts and pains, toxic relationships, and other painful situations we've been holding on to for weeks, months, and possibly years. We have been feverishly praying that God would take it away. Maybe our prayers even included a declaration, "God please take this away, because this is holding me down." Yet, God is saying, "If you give it up, I will take it up." It is up to YOU to stamp your issues and raise your arms in submission to signal to God that you have problems that need to be handed over to Him. God will pick up your issues, but He will also leave you some. The mail God leaves is peace, joy, patience, love, and other good mail that does not cost money, but obedience! Now is the time to admit you have issues and they need to be sent out.

Even Jesus Asked Questions

"After three days they found him (Jesus) in the temple courts, sitting among the teachers, listening to them and <u>asking them questions.</u>"

— Luke 2:46 (NIV)

Have you ever been in a situation where the discussion taking place around you was totally above your head? The conversation is interesting to say the least, you desire to participate, but you have no knowledge about the topic being discussed. Have you ever been in Sunday School class or Bible study and a question arises in your mind, but you don't want to look stupid by asking it? The desire to find the answer(s) burns within you, but you are too proud to raise your hand and/or just ask the question.

Many of us struggle with ignorance as it relates to certain things. However, there is absolutely nothing wrong with not knowing something. The reality is that the only way to obtain an answer is to ask a question. This sounds simple and it is something we all know; however, we still find it difficult to do what seems to be a simple thing. A former teacher made a statement, "The only dumb question is the question that is not asked." We struggle with this in school, the community, the workplace, and even in church. Obviously, in the midst of the teachers, there was something mentioned or talked about in which Jesus said to himself, "I don't know" — so even JESUS unashamedly asked the teachers questions. We, too, must humble ourselves and learn to ask questions of those who have the knowledge we seek. It feels good to know that even Jesus asked questions, so we should not be too prideful to do the same.

What's For You, Is For You!

"...What He opens, no one can shut, and what He shuts no one can open. I know your deeds. See I have placed before you an open door than no one can shut. I know you have little strength, yet you have kept my word and have not denied my name."

— *Revelation 3:7-8 (NIV)*

One afternoon, at work, I was craving a Snickers candy bar. I made my trek to the vending machine to satisfy my craving. When I arrived at the vending machine, there were sticky notes posted on the front by people who had lost their money in the machine that day. There were several notes on the machine, and all had lost money ranging from $0.50 - $1. I looked at the notes and thought to myself, *Do I want to put my money in here and take the chance on losing it after seeing others have lost their money today?* After a few moments, I made a decision not to allow the experience of the note posters to determine my outcome. Therefore, I inserted my money and retrieved the Snickers I had been craving. I could have forfeited my treat if I had given too much attention to the notes.

Maybe there is something in particular you have been craving from God. Despite your longing, you have become doubtful because you are paying attention to the note posters around you. Someone more qualified than you applied for the position you desire, so you draw the conclusion that you will not get the job. Maybe you know someone who had an undesirable experience/outcome with the illness you now have, so you wonder if you will have the same experience.

31

Someone you thought to be smart was unsuccessful in college, therefore, you question if you can be successful. This list is endless. Nevertheless, when you begin to do mental and emotional somersaults, you must make a decision not to allow their notes to distract you from your treat. The outcome of their experience cannot dictate the outcome of yours. Therefore, continue to insert your desires and prayers into the hands of God and retrieve that which God has for you. What God has for you, it is for you — and only you!

True Worship

*"God is a Spirit: and they that worship him must worship
him in spirit and in truth."*

—*John 4:24 (KJV)*

As a Baptist youth pastor, I was asked to minister to youth of
another denomination. I gladly accepted the invitation, but
as the day approached, I began to get nervous. I was nervous
because I did not know how people of that denomination
worshipped. I did not know if they jumped, shouted, ran
down the aisles, or worshipped quietly within themselves.
As I prayed about it, I was reminded of the fact that it did
not matter how they worshipped, but rather Who they
worshipped.

There are points where we become so preoccupied with
the way others worship that we overlook the true meaning of
worship. Worship is our response to God for who He is and
what He has done for us expressed in and by the things we
do, say, and most of all, the way we live. Therefore, there are
many ways one can worship. If an individual does not shout
to the top of their lungs, it does not suggest a lack of worship.
Conversely, because a person *does* shout, run, and/or dance,
it is not an indication of unpretentious worship. God is to be
worshipped in spirit and truth. No specific method is specified
in the Bible. There are many different denominations in the
body of Christ. No matter the Christian denomination, we
all have the same responsibility and that is to worship God
in spirit and truth. Do not allow yourself to feel as if you are
not a true worshiper of God because your mode of worship is
different from that of other people.

Smile! You're On Camera

"You have searched me, Lord, and you know me. You know when I sit and when I rise; you perceive my thoughts from afar. You discern my going out and my lying down; you are familiar with all my ways. Before a word is on my tongue you, Lord, know it completely."

- Psalm 139:1-4 (NIV)

One day, while exiting the mall, I noticed people running, shouting, and crowding around a news reporter and his cameraman. People did all kinds of antics trying to be noticed by the camera. Some jumped up and down behind the reporter, some made loud outbursts, and some even jumped in front of the reporter. The common denominator was that everyone wanted to be captured by the camera. Everyone wanted to be on TV so that people who viewed the nightly news may call them and declare, "I saw (heard) you on TV last night." It was amazing to witness the lengths people would go to while trying to be noticed by the camera.

Have you ever considered the fact that God is always watching us? What if God said to you, "I saw (heard) you last night?" Are you as excited to be captured by God's camera as some are for the nightly news? Some of us cringe at the thought of things we did and said that were captured on God's camera. God has seen some of us in places we should not be in and He has heard things that were not godlike. Therefore, we are not so quick to go to such great lengths to be on God's camera. Nevertheless, the camera is always on! When talking to your children, know that God's camera is always on. When speaking (or not speaking) to co-workers, know that God's camera is always on. When in the car or grocery store, know that His camera is always on. Smile, you're on God's camera — even at this moment!

Riding With No Hands

"Trust in the LORD with all your heart and lean not on your own understanding; in all your ways submit to him, and he will make your paths straight."

- Proverbs 3:5-6 (NIV)

When I was growing up, every child had the goal of learning to ride a bicycle. Eventually, there was a transition from training wheels to being able to ride alone. Of course, when one wanted to boast, he/she would ride the bicycle with no hands. They would release the handlebars, continue to peddle, and place the hands somewhere else — but never on the handlebars. It was every child's goal to be able to ride a bicycle with no hands.

Life's journey with God is much like riding a bicycle. There are training wheels phases and then there are phases of life in which we feel comfortable riding alone. This is the point where you no longer depend on the advice of others, but you are able to arrive at your own conclusions about what to do or say. However, there are times when you feel so comfortable riding alone that no one else should have the handlebars to your life. You should not receive their input, guidance, or any unsolicited advice.

Sometimes you want to drive your own life, you want to please *yourself*. No one wants to experience the gray areas of life where you don't know what to do, where to go, or what to say. These are the stints when you are doing the best you can, all to no avail. It is during these times that you should release the handlebars, pedal with prayer, and ride on God's promises. There are and will be situations life will take you to in which you must totally depend on God. The key is to TOTALLY depend and ride with God — with no hands!

Become the Picture on the Box

"And we know that in ALL things God works for the good of those who love him, who have been called according to his purpose."

— *Romans 8:28 (NIV)*

When looking for a puzzle, oftentimes one makes the determination to purchase it based on the picture on the box. There are many pieces within to create the picture on the box. It takes time and effort to put all the pieces together in order to complete the puzzle. Occasionally, the picture on the box is placed nearby in order to monitor our progress. Some pieces of the puzzle may be small, big, and at times look even identical to another piece. In the end, they all fit together to create the picture on the box.

Life is like a puzzle; God has a picture of what He wants us to be. The many experiences you are having, or have had, are the pieces God is going to use, or is using, to complete the picture He has for you. There are some things you must go through that are nothing short of unpleasant. You may have a past you are ashamed of. There have been things to happen in, around, and to you that you do not understand. In fact, there are moments when you begin to think they are of no use to God because too much has taken place in your life. You must know that everything that has happened in your life are the pieces to complete God's puzzle for you. God has a picture of you in mind as He monitors your progress. God uses ALL things (the good, the bad, and the ugly), for our good. No matter what you have gone through, what you are going through, or will go through, know that they are pieces needed for you to become the picture on God's puzzle box.

It Does Not Fit

"For I know the plans I have for you, declares the LORD, plans to prosper you and not to harm you, plans to give you hope and a future."

— Jeremiah 29:11 (NIV)

While in a department store one weekend, I was looking for a pair of dress shoes when I came across a pair I felt were just right. They were the right color, style, and on sale for the right price. However, when I asked the sales associate for my shoe size, she only had the shoe two sizes smaller than what I needed. The problem was that I really wanted the shoes! Because I really wanted the shoes, I tried one of them on, stretched it, and attempted to squeeze my foot in it, until finally I had to accept the fact that they were too small. The color, style, and price were perfect, but I had to accept the reality the shoes simply did not fit.

In our lives, we come across people and situations that seem perfect. The situation or person perfectly fits your set of ideals. The person is a Christian, physically attractive, has a good job, drives a nice car, has a nice home — you believe this has to be the person for you! You have a job offer with a great salary, excellent benefits, Monday-Friday, travel privileges — of course, this has to be the job for you! Oftentimes, you can come across situations that appear flawless, but you know deep within that something is missing. In order to fill the void, you are tempted to stretch it by ignoring the lack of peace you have and you attempt to squeeze past what you know to be true. You think to yourself, *I think I can get past this or that.* After you have tried to stretch and squeeze the person/situation into what you desire, you finally have to accept that it does not fit.

The truth is that sometimes it is difficult to trust God for better when you feel already you have the best. If we are really honest, you can even feel as if God is doing you an injustice or simply being unfair. Nevertheless, God's ultimate plans are to prosper, not to cause harm. The reality is that what/who you have is maybe two (or more) sizes smaller than what/who God has purposed for you. God knows who and what is best for you to give you a hope and a future. Don't stretch and squeeze any longer, but accept the reality that it does not fit.

No Audible

"For my thoughts are not your thoughts, neither are your ways my ways," declares the Lord. "As the heavens are higher than the earth, so are my ways higher than your ways and my thoughts than your thoughts."

— Isaiah 55:8-9 (NIV)

"Trust in the Lord with all your heart and lean not on your own understanding; in all your ways submit to him, and he will make your paths straight."

— Proverbs 3:5-6 (NIV)

In the game of football, each team has an offensive coordinator who calls the plays that should be run on the field. However, occasionally the quarterback will call an *audible,* meaning he is overriding the call of the offensive coordinator and institutes a play of his own. Oftentimes, the audible results in an interception or something else that turns the ball over to the other team. Needless to say, the offensive coordinator often gets upset because the quarterback chose to change what he called. It is the desire of the offensive coordinator to run the play with no audible. The offensive coordinator is perched high in the press box, and therefore has a view of the field that is different from the view on the field. Because he has a higher view, he knows what plays need to be run and when they should be run.

There are times in life that God, the Offensive Coordinator, calls plays in our lives we don't want to run or live out. He calls us to do and experience things we are uncomfortable with or simply do not wish to do. When we hear the call, we sometimes override what God said thereby we turn things over to ourselves. Let's face it, when we think we have the answers and try to control our own lives, we are destined to lose. Not only is God our Creator, but He has a higher view of our lives than we do. Therefore, we must be confident God knows what He is doing despite how uncomfortable, difficult, and arduous life can be; we have to run the play (do what He says, walk through it) with no audible.

Know Who You Are

"You dear children, are from God and have overcome them, because the one who is in you is greater than the one who is in the world."

— *I John 4:4 (NIV)*

A young man was flying to Tulsa, Oklahoma to give a presentation to a group of corporate managers. During the flight, he began to get nervous, thinking and wondering, *I hope I do well, I pray I speak clearly, I hope I don't stutter, I am too young for this, Am I really qualified to do this?* and other thoughts of doubt that came to his mind. His hands began to sweat as he squirmed to a more comfortable position (as if changing his physical position would change his mental position), then he heard a small voice speak to him and say, "Do you know who you are?" He sat confused and said to himself, "Of course, I am Cameron Walker."

Of course, being an omniscient (all-knowing) God, He began to elaborate on His initial question. "You are not just Cameron Walker, but you are MY child." God began to pour Scriptures into his mind to give him peace about the doubts running through his mind. "I can do ALL things through Christ which strengthens me," (Philippians 4:13). "No weapon formed against me shall prosper," (Isaiah 54:17). These are just a few Scriptures, in addition to today's text, that God used to bring comfort and assurance to Cameron. As the Holy Spirit began to minister to him, his anxiety was IMMEDIATELY erased!

Have you ever been worried about an upcoming job interview, public presentation, test, or just being in the midst of unfamiliar people? You begin to question yourself, *What if I don't get the job? What if I stutter when I talk? What if I fail the test? What will 'they' think of me? Do I have what it takes?* I urge you to hide today's text and other Scriptures in your heart when the enemy attempts to plant negative or doubtful thoughts in your mind. You are God's child and God wants the BEST for you! You can never leave the presence of God, so never hesitate to call on Him ... God declares, "Lo I am with you always even to the end of the age" (Matt. 28:20). Know who you are!

Don't Take the Alternate Route

"Now to him who is able to do immeasurably more than all that we ask or imagine, according to his power that is at work within us ..."

— *Ephesians 3:20 (NIV)*

One night a friend and I were driving home from a rival basketball game. As we walked through the crowd on the way to the car, I began to ponder which route I would take to avoid traffic. Of course, I chose the route I thought no one else would take. When I took the "*For Tim only*" route and approached my exit, it seemed that everyone else chose the same route! My first thought was to turn around and take another route. However, I decided to remain where I was and endure what I thought to be a traffic nightmare. To my surprise, the traffic moved smoothly and did not last as long as I thought it would. What I thought to be a traffic jam, turned out to be my freeway!

There are times in life that resemble traffic jams. Things look difficult from afar and you really want to take an alternate route. Most times in traffic jams, the alternate route is to not take one at all! We treat traffic jams as we would a class that many consider to be impossible to pass. We take the "alternate route" and decide not to take the class. If a job seems too hard to do, we take the alternate route and don't apply for the position. If there are marital or relationship troubles, we take the alternate route and refuse to come to some resolve. There are many situations that cause us to consider alternate routes. However, when you trust God, by getting and staying IN the traffic jam, you will watch God see you through. What you first think is a traffic jam, God will turn it into your freeway. Don't run from your situation, but rather run IN your situation, "for nothing is impossible with God" (Luke 1:37)! Don't take the alternate route!

Advertise God

"You are the light of the world. A town built on a hill cannot be hidden. Neither do people light a lamp and put it under a bowl. Instead they put it on its stand, and it gives light to everyone in the house. In the same way, let your light shine before others, that they may see your good deeds and glorify your Father in heaven."

— Matthew 5:14-16 (NIV)

It is no secret that advertising is important in getting people to buy into a particular product or concept. On my job, I find that the company's cafeteria has an interesting method of advertising. At the entrance of the cafeteria, there are examples of the featured dishes for the day. One day I looked at the featured dishes and said to myself, *The Chicken Rueben looks good, I wonder what it tastes like, so I think that is what I want.* Looking at the example made me curious as to what it would be like to taste it. Needless to say, I bought the Chicken Rueben and it tasted better than it looked.

Light is something that is seen. God has commissioned believers to be the light of the world. We are to be light in every area of our lives. When people see you, they should see the light of God. To the unsaved, you may look or sound different, but to the saved, you resemble light. When people are in your space, there should be something different about you that causes people to say to themselves, "He/she looks or acts different, I wonder what their life is like... I think that life is what I want." The lifestyle you live should make people curious of what it means to have a relationship with God. When people see the light of your character, you are advertising your relationship with God. The hope is they will taste it by buying into it. After they try God for themselves, they will realize that a life in God's family tastes better than it looks. Advertise God today.

He Didn't Give Up On You

"Bear with each other and forgive one another if any of you has a grievance against someone. Forgive as the Lord forgave you."

— *Colossians 3:13 (NIV)*

Has someone done or said something to you to hurt you to the point where it was difficult to release? The person you thought would never hurt you was the very one to cause you pain. The person you thought you could trust was the person who betrayed you. When this happens, the first thing we say is, "I am finished with him/her," "I cannot believe he/she would do that to me," or "I trusted him/her only for them to betray me." That person no longer receives phone calls, visits, birthday gifts, Christmas gifts, etc. because of something they did or said (possibly one thing) to cause us pain.

When we consider the hurt we have sustained, we must view them through the lens of the many times we have betrayed God. How many times has He felt He could trust you only to find out that He couldn't? You could not count the number of times you know you let God down. Can you imagine Him saying, "I cannot believe (insert your name here) did that to me!" Nevertheless, God continues to love and provide for you as if you have done nothing. You can clearly recall many occasions when you have hurt God, but God never said, "I am finished with (your name)." What if God ceased to answer your calls in prayer, pay you early morning visits, and give you gifts because of a hurt you caused? If God forgave you on the basis in which you forgive others, you would lack much. Therefore, you must forgive and love those who hurt you just as God loves and forgives you. The next time someone hurts you and you feel like giving up on him or her, remember God didn't give up on you.

Order in the Court!

"Fools show their annoyance at once, but the prudent overlook an insult."

— Proverbs 12:16 (NIV)

"In you, Lord my God, I put my trust. I trust in you; do not let me be put to shame, nor let my enemies triumph over me. No one who hopes in you will ever be put to shame, but shame will come on those who are treacherous without cause."

— Psalm 25:1-3 (NIV)

Court shows have become very popular over the past couple decades. On one court show, the people in the court became disorderly following a defendant's response to something the plaintiff said. It was clear that those in the background disagreed with the defendant's response based on the plaintiff's accusations. Based on what was said, the people in the background joined forces with the plaintiff. As a result of their alliance, they began to get noisy, make loud outbursts, and hurl insults at the defendant. As the outbursts and insults were hurled, the defendant stood still and speechless. After a short time, the judge yelled, "Order in the court!" Immediately after the judge's proclamation, peace was restored to the courtroom. At the conclusion of the case, the defendant was found not guilty and the people in the background were ashamed.

There is nothing like feeling like a defendant in the courtroom of life. Nothing you say or do is accepted, everything you say and do is wrong, and it seems virtually everyone around you wishes to see you fail because of the accusations from the accusers in your life. The accusers can range from people on the job, school, family, community, and maybe even church. In response to the accusations, remain still and speechless and allow God to fight your battle. Be prepared for the disagreement and maybe greater opposition from your accusers who cannot fathom such a response. As the insults are hurled and the accusations continue, hold your ground, for in a short while, God will proclaim order, while the plaintiffs and people in the background stand ashamed.

Remove the Band-Aid

"Humble yourselves, therefore, under God's mighty hand, that he may lift you up in due time. Cast ALL your anxiety on him because he cares for you."

— *I Peter 5:6-7 (NIV)*

A little boy was at the playground when he fell and wounded himself. He placed a Band-Aid on the wound in hopes that no one would see it and that it would completely heal. After some time of having the Band-Aid, the little boy discovered the Band-Aid was perfect for covering the wound, but no healing was taking place. After speaking with his mother, she advised him to remove the Band-Aid, expose it to the air, and assured him that the wound would heal. When the Band-Aid was removed, the little boy's wound began to heal.

Do you need healing? Could you be placing Band-Aids on long-term wounds that remain open? Maybe you have a wound of being abandoned as a child. Maybe you have a Band-Aid to cover up the wound associated with childhood, a previous relationship, or situation. There are many wounds that can be covered up, but not healed.

For years on end, the wounds are covered with pseudo assurances such as, *I have blocked it out, I am not worried about it, it's over and I am past it,* etc. Statements of this kind are nothing short of Band-Aids. One of the worst things a person can do is attempt to walk through life with Band-Aids in an effort to put things behind, but the pain still remains — even subliminally. Know that God cares about your hurts, if you are courageous enough to be honest with yourself, remove the Band-Aid, expose them to Him and your healing will begin to take place.

Do Your Duty

"Now all has been heard; here is the conclusion of the matter: Fear God and keep his commandments, for this is the whole duty of mankind."

— Ecclesiastes 12:13 (NIV)

There are many duties we must perform on a daily basis. Some fulfill the duties of a parent, spouse, employee, church leader, friend, or other duties all in one day. As a parent, you know when the duty of a parent is necessary. As an employee, church leader, or community leader there are specific duties. The duties performed are based on where you are, who you are around, or what needs to be done. Whatever the situation, you know which duty to perform.

Christians have one duty to perform on a daily basis - to keep God's commandments. In addition to performing the duties of a parent, spouse, employee, church leader, or friend, there is an ultimate duty that must be performed. It is vital that amid all of your obligations that you do not neglect your duty to fear God and keep his commandments in order to perform other duties. This is your *whole duty* no matter where you are, who you are around, or what needs to be done. Whatever the situation, do your duty!

Maintain the Solid Side

"...Let your light shine before others, that they may see your good deeds and glorify your Father in heaven."

— *Matthew 5:16 (NIV)*

"Rejoice always, pray continually, give thanks in all circumstances; for this is God's will for you in Christ Jesus."

— *I Thessalonians 5:16-18 (NIV)*

As I watched a truck back into the driveway, I looked underneath the truck and noticed there was something on the tires. It appeared as if the driver bought tires with the something on them for a cheaper price, but installed them on the truck on the opposite side so only the solid side would show. The only way to see what was on the other side of the tires was if the truck was parked or moving slowly. The owner obviously did not want people to see what was on the tires, he desired that people only see the solid side. Nevertheless, when the truck slowed down or parked, anyone could see what the driver did not want to be revealed.

Have you ever come across a Christian who behaves a certain way in some situations and differently in others? Have you ever watched how their conversation and character changes with the environment? In church, there is the solid side — the ultimate Christian. However, in the grocery store or mall, you see and hear something else. Some put up the façade so that only the solid side shows in certain situations, but when life slows down, you see and hear something else. As believers, we must be careful not to be uncertain and vacillating, even when life seems to slow down or we feel parked and at a standstill. People are watching you, especially when the chips are down. You must be careful to maintain the solid side of hope in God and not allow your circumstances to allow people to see something else.

Be Ready When He Gets Back

"Now, brothers and sisters, about times and dates we do not need to write to you, for you know very well that the day of the Lord will come like a thief in the night."

— *I Thessalonians 5:1-3 (NIV)*

While watching television one evening, the words "High Terror Threat" streamed across the bottom of the screen. This message served as a notice to everyone watching television that there was a possibility of a terrorist attack and to take the necessary precautions to be ready. In mainly every area of life, contingency plans are in place for situations ranging from fires to terrorist attacks. A contingency plan describes exactly what to do in case of an emergency. If one studies the contingency plan and puts the suggested items into practice, this person will be well-prepared for an emergency.

Each day we live, there is a possibility of Jesus' return. We sometimes take for granted that the *threat level* of His coming is high. However, the coming of Christ is a definite fact, not a mere threat. Knowing this, believers should take the necessary precautions by living in accordance to God's Word to be ready at all times. The Bible is our contingency plan, it describes exactly what to do in the meantime before Jesus comes back. If we do this, we will be ready for His coming. Are you ready?

It's Forgotten

"You will again have compassion on us; you will tread our sins underfoot and hurl all our iniquities into the depths of the sea."

— *Micah 7:19 (NIV)*

"... As far as the east is from the west, so far has he removed our transgressions from us."

—*Psalm 103:12 (NIV)*

In the hills of a small county in Mississippi, there was a little boy who enjoyed throwing stones as far as he could from the bank into the river. This was something he enjoyed so much that he did it on an everyday basis. Each day he would throw stones into the river for a period of time and walk away unconcerned about the effect of the stones on the river or its inhabitants. Over the summer, many stones were thrown, but they never washed back onto the bank.

Each day we all have stones of sin that need to be confessed (thrown) to God and repented about. This is something that should be done on a regular basis. Often times, some confess and repent of sins, but hang on to them. Some beat themselves up over things done or said months or years ago. One must be reminded that the confession and repentance of sin is like throwing stones into the river of God. Each day there are stones of sin to throw, but they never wash back onto the bank. You must work hard not to allow anyone or anything to negatively wash back onto the bank of your life.

Much as the river accepts and retains thrown stones, God forgives and forgets thrown sins. Whatever sinful things you have done or said - confess, repent, and know it's forgotten.

Playtime is Over

"... If my people, who are called by my name, will humble themselves and pray and seek my face and turn from their wicked ways, then will I hear from heaven and will forgive their sin and will heal their land."

— *II Chronicles 7:14 (NIV)*

I went to a local elementary school to visit with a friend who taught at the school. When I arrived at the school, her students were playing outdoors during their physical education time. After the children played for a while, the teacher then walked to the middle of the playground and raised her hand. When the students noticed her raised hand, they stopped playing and immediately began to get in line behind the teacher. The teacher's raised hand was a signal to the students that it was time to stop playing and get in line, because playtime is over.

Over the years, we have witnessed a number of tragedies that have shaken the world. We have witnessed terrorist attacks, earthquakes, hurricanes, political, social, and racial unrest that have impacted the lives of thousands of people. Based on what we are seeing throughout our country and the world, God's Hand is raised as a signal to His children to stop playing and get in line.

In many ways, the people of God have been playing by silently sitting idle and watching terrible things take place in the world, communities and homes. Now is the time for believers to humble ourselves, pray, seek His face, turn from our wicked ways for God to heal our land. There is no time for playing, but plenty of time for praying. Playtime is over!

Don't Miss It

"But the Lord said to Samuel, 'Do not consider his appearance or his height, for I have rejected him. The Lord does not look at the things people look at. People look at the outward appearance, but the Lord looks at the heart.'"

— *I Samuel 16:7 (NIV)*

One of our family traditions is that my wife and I do an Easter egg hunt at our home for our kids. We use eggs of various sizes and place candy and other little trinkets inside of them. They look forward to our Jackson Easter egg hunt and they all search in hopes of finding what they deem to be the "golden egg." The egg may not be gold in color, but the golden egg is the egg that has money inside of it. My wife and I stand back as the kids excitedly accumulate eggs and place them into their containers. One year, Avery saw a large decorative egg in her view, and she ran to get it because she was certain it had to be the golden egg because of its size and its appearance. She was shocked to discover that despite the beauty and size of the egg, it was empty, but a regular egg in her basket contained the money she desired.

Oftentimes, we misjudge people and things on the basis of size and outward appearance. When we do this, we often find that something or someone can have great size and great beauty, but is empty on the inside. In judging the value, or lack thereof, based on aesthetics alone, we often miss or miscalculate the value of what appears to be regular. Don't miss it.

Ignoring the Caller ID

"Here I am! I stand at the door and knock. If anyone hears my voice and opens the door, I will come in and eat with that person, and they with me."

— *Revelation 3:20 (NIV)*

The development of caller ID was revolutionary in how or if we answer calls. When someone calls us, we almost involuntarily look at the caller ID before answering. After assessing the number noted on the caller ID display, we decide whether we will answer the call or not. There are times when the caller ID denotes "unknown name," or "unknown number." Most times, these are calls we do not answer. However, there are other instances in which we know exactly who the caller is, but purposely neglect to answer the phone.

Reasons vary as to why we choose not to answer the phone, but most times we do not answer because we know what they are going to talk about. In today's society, we have a choice to answer or not answer. Nevertheless, for those of us who are old enough to remember life before the development of caller ID, we had no choice, but to answer all calls because we never knew who was calling.

Have you ever heard God calling you to do or say something in particular? God told you exactly what to do - go here, go there, call this person, talk to that person, etc. Often times, you hear the divine phone ringing and it is God calling you to do certain things. Your heart (the spiritual caller ID) confirms it's a call of God, yet sometimes you choose not to answer. Reasons (or excuses) vary as to why God's calls go unanswered. One reason why you do not answer is because you know precisely what the call is about. In this moment, revisit the time when caller ID was not available. When God calls, answer, listen to, and do what He says.

Tell God What You Want

"Do not be anxious about anything, but in every situation, by prayer and petition, with thanksgiving, present your requests to God."

- Philippians 4:6 (NIV)

One night in the drive-thru of a local fast food restaurant, I placed my order for a cheeseburger and fries. After placing my order, I made a mental note to ask for extra ketchup. As I slowly moved through the line and reached the pick-up window, I noticed a sticker on the window that said, "Condiments upon request." The sticker was their way of letting me know that if I wanted ketchup, I would have to ask for it because they would not voluntarily give it to me. The ketchup was always available, but if I neglected to request it, I would forfeit the opportunity to have it.

There are many things we desire in life. Wisdom, cars, homes, better jobs, and help with situations are just a few desired requests. Many times, those desires are discussed with other people, but not presented to God. We tell people, "I want this," "I want that," "It would be nice if..." We tell people as if they can and/or will provide us with the things we want or desire. There may be some things you desire that seemingly everyone (except God) knows about.

Today, you must know there are things God wants to do for you that will only be done after your requests have been made known. Of course, God does not bless you with things that are not in His will, but at least He will know what desires you have. In the words of the late Rev. Laurence Hudson, a "Prayer that is not prayed is a prayer that is not answered." Tell God what you want.

Shut Down the Old System

"Therefore, if anyone is in Christ, the new creation has come: The old has gone, the new is here!"

— *II Corinthians 5:17 (NIV)*

There are many free programs that are offered to computer users to install on their personal computers. One day, after installing a program on my personal computer, a window appeared that stated, "Installation completed, computer must restart to begin using the program." The computer would then shut down and restart with the new program functioning. Apparently, the only way the new program would function correctly is if the system was first shut down.

When an individual gives their life to Christ, they are asking God to install divine software into their lives. In order for the godly software to take effect, one must shut down the old system. The old system may include unhealthy places once frequented, the relinquishment of old habits, toxic relationships, etc. Godly software includes a godly way of doing things, a renewed way of thinking, a new way of relating to people, the development of new habits, and a host of other things God installs into the lives of believers. It can be tempting people to make an attempt to operate God's programs while holding onto the old system. As with computers, godly software cannot function appropriately until you shut down the old system.

Make An Impression

"And you also were included in Christ when you heard the message of truth, the gospel of your salvation. When you believed, you were marked in him with a seal, the promised Holy Spirit."

- Ephesians 1:13 (NIV)

Many government agencies place a seal on certain documents. The seal is used to make the document an "official" government document. When one opens an envelope containing the document, the seal is the first thing you'll notice. In addition to the fact that the seal is very visible, if one rubs their fingers across the seal, the impression of the seal can be felt.

When a person comes to Christ, he or she is marked in him with a seal, the promised Holy Spirit. This seal of the Holy Spirit brands a person as an *official* child of the Kingdom. The seal of the Holy Spirit in your life should be visible in how you live and be felt to a point where people see and feel the impression of God in your life. Sometimes you wonder why people say things like, "There is something about you. "You don't act like everyone else," or "I admire the way you carry yourself." Statements like this and others of the kind should let you know your life exhibits God's seal. Your seal of the Holy Spirit has made and should make a godly impression on the lives of other people.

Let It Go

"Cast your cares on the LORD and he will sustain you; he will never let the righteous be shaken."

— Psalm 55:22 (NIV)

After having a sweater for a few years, a young man reached a point where he was tired of wearing it. The young man's friend offered to take the sweater off his hands to which he agreed. However, when the day came for the young man to give his friend the sweater, he handed it to him and said, "Here you go, you can have it," but he didn't let it go. He and his friend were in a tug-o-war with the sweater that the young man had said he wanted to give up. Though he said he wanted to give it up, he did not want to let it go when the time came.

After a little more tug-o-war, his friend finally said, "If you are going to let me have the sweater, you have to let it go." It seems the young man had become so accustomed to having the sweater that he did not want to let go of what he said he wanted to rid himself of. Finally, the young man decided to allow his friend to have the sweater, and the friend received it gladly.

Oftentimes, you have situations or troubles in your life that you say you want to be rid of. You have a Friend in Jesus who has offered to take ALL troubles off your hands. However, we oftentimes say to the Friend, "Here you go, you can have my troubles," but we do not let them go. In many cases, letting go is difficult because over time, you become accustomed to dealing with things on your own. In fact, if you are honest, you can admit that your handling of life's challenges and troubles did not yield any significant improvements. My brother, my sister, you have a Friend who is anxiously waiting to take them away from you. It is up to you to cast on the Lord everything that concerns or troubles you and God will gladly receive it all. Let it go!

Promise Keeper

"...What I have said, that will I bring about; what I have planned, that will I do."

— Isaiah 46:11 (NIV)

"The one who calls you is faithful, and he will do it."

— I Thessalonians 5:24 (NIV)

There was a little boy who loved to fish, and his father told him that he would take him fishing. Days, weeks and months passed, and the little boy began to wonder if his father was going to do what he said he would do. He never said anything to his father, but he said to himself, *If Daddy said he would do it; he's going to do it.* After a while, the day came when the father fulfilled the promise to his son to take him fishing. The little boy was excited about the fact that his father was fulfilling his wish.

There have been some things you have prayed about and asked God for. Your spirit bears witness that those things will come to pass. However, years have passed, and you are still holding on to the hope that God will fulfill His promise. To your dismay, sometimes you are literally watching others receive healing, deliverance, prosperity, provision, and other things you may have requested of God. Child of God, if God said He would do it, He is going to do it. After a while, the day WILL come when you will get just what He promised you. You can get excited today about the fact that God is about to fulfill your wishes! God is a PROMISE KEEPER!

It's Okay to Rest

"By the seventh day God had finished the work he had been doing; so on the seventh day he rested from all his work."

— Genesis 2:2 (NIV)

Do you ever feel like there is always something to do and no time to rest? You have to do this, do that, take the kids here, there, go here, go there, attend this meeting. Sound familiar? You feel like your life is all work. My brother, my sister, God never meant for our lives to be all work, no play, or no rest. Of course, you love your children, but when do you take time for yourself? I know you love ministry, but when do you take time for yourself? You love your job, but when do you rest?

In Genesis 1-2:2, God worked for six consecutive days, but "On the seventh day he rested from all his work." God took time to rest and be rejuvenated. Jesus did not heal people 24/7. In fact, there are several points throughout the Bible when Jesus stopped, drew away from everyone (including the disciples) to go up on the mountainside BY HIMSELF. Jesus' moments of isolation serve as a great example for believers. From time to time (even for a short time), there needs to be time away from the spouse, children, school, work, or ministry that you use to rest. If Jesus took time to be alone and rest, we should do the same. There is nothing spiritual or healthy about working continuously without adequate rest. Take some time to rest — Jesus did!

Preparation is Key

"Therefore put on the full armor of God, so that when the day of evil comes, you may be able to stand your ground, and after you have done everything, to stand. Stand firm then, with the belt of truth buckled around your waist, with the breastplate of righteousness in place, and with your feet fitted with the readiness that comes from the gospel of peace. In addition to all this, take up the shield of faith, with which you can extinguish all the flaming arrows of the evil one. Take the helmet of salvation and the sword of the Spirit, which is the word of God."

— Ephesians 6:13-17 (NIV)

Many people walk through their neighborhood as a form of exercise. In my neighborhood, I see a variety of walkers. Some walk fast, slow, or at a moderate pace. Some walk one mile, two miles, three miles, or even more. Some walk alone or with a group. There are many things that differentiate each walker from others. However, the one thing I have found to be common is the carrying of some form of stick. The type of *stick* can range from a tree branch to a golf club. The stick is used to fend off any aggressive pets that may threaten the health and welfare of the walkers walking through the neighborhood. Each walker never knows if or when they will be attacked, however, each carries a stick in preparation.

In our walk through the neighborhood of life, we never know when we may be attacked by the enemy. As with neighborhood walkers, the attacks can come out of nowhere and we have to be prepared to fend off the attacker(s). The body of Christ is made up of people of different races, sizes, ages, levels of education, and many other things that differentiate believers from one another. Each day you live, there is a great possibility you will be attacked in some way whether at work, home, at the grocer, the mall, or even at church! However, there should be one thing in common for all believers. We should all be carrying a stick, the sword of the Spirit, which is the word of God. The sword is used to fend off temptations and attacks of the enemy. You never know when you will be attacked, be familiar with the sword because preparation is key.

Leave It Alone

"... For I know the plans I have for you," declares the LORD, "plans to prosper you and not to harm you, plans to give you hope and a future."

— Jeremiah 29:11 (NIV)

"Now to him who is able to do immeasurably more than all we ask or imagine, according to his power that is at work within us ..."

— Ephesians 3:20 (NIV)

As children, we learned many nursery rhymes. One that stands out in my mind is "Humpty Dumpty."

Humpty Dumpty sat on a wall; Humpty Dumpty had a great fall. All the king's horses and all the king's men, couldn't put Humpty together again.

Humpty Dumpty was something (someone) who easily broke when it fell. Someone obviously wanted to put Humpty Dumpty back together. However, after many efforts, it could not be done. Therefore, Humpty Dumpty remained broken.

Life can place you in some Humpty Dumpty situations. You can have broken relationships you want to put back together again. You can have a broken job you want to put back together again. Obviously there are a number of things that can be named, and the truth is, there are many broken conditions in our lives that we (and others) have tried to put back together, but were unsuccessful. The hard truth is acknowledging that some situations are better broken than they are fixed. The relationship or friendship you desire is sometimes not the relationship that is the healthiest.

The job you desire to remain in is sometimes not God's will for you. Over time, we have adapted our lives to the old adage, "If it ain't broke, don't fix it." However, in certain circumstances, God declares, "If it's broke, leave it broke, and don't try to fix it." If you mess with what God is trying to do, you will mess it up! God's intent is to give you the best — better than you could ever imagine.

It's Okay

"He is our father in the sight of God, in whom he believed – the God who gives life to the dead and calls into being things that were not."

— Romans 4:17 (NIV)

"...for he is the kind of person who is always thinking about the cost."

— Proverbs 23:7 (NIV)

The Mid-South Fair comes to the city of Memphis each year with a variety of rides, games, food, exhibits, and booths. While at the fair one night, I saw a young man walk around with what was determined to be his *dog*. Interestingly, this dog was only a long, stiff leash with a collar. I watched the young man as he talked to this *dog* and I remember thinking, "He is talking as if a real dog is on the leash." However, the young man was not concerned about the many people around him who probably thought he was crazy for talking to something that was not there in reality.

There are many situations we have to speak life into even when they are dead in reality. We must speak financial freedom in spite of debt. Speak healing in spite of the diagnosis. Speak provision in spite of lack. Speak deliverance of loved ones, in spite of their worldliness. Speak success into the marriage in spite of the turmoil. Many situations and circumstances in our lives look impossible, but we must speak to and about them as if the situation were the opposite. Like the young man, we cannot be concerned about those around us who may think we are crazy for speaking life into situations that appear dead. Right now, the situation you are in may not be okay in reality, but speak to it as if it is okay – and it will be okay!

Wait on the Lord

"Even youths grow tired and weary, and young men stumble and fall; but those who hope in the Lord will renew their strength. They will soar on wings like eagles; they will run and not grow weary, they will walk and not be faint."

— *Isaiah 40:30-31 (NIV)*

In order for one's strength to be renewed, one must first wait on the Lord. We desire the strength to handle life's challenges, but we sometimes find ourselves in a weak state declaring, "I have done all I can do, I don't know what else to do, I feel like giving up, I am tired of this." Amid the litany of declarations, God is saying, "Now that YOU have done all you can do, YOU don't know what else to do, YOU feel like giving up, YOU are tired, when will you wait on ME?"

The truth is that sometimes weakness is the result of a refusal to wait. You feel you have been faithful to God and have done the things He has asked you to do, and you do not understand why things continue to be the way they are. It is an enormous mistake to assume that waiting on God is wasting time, rather than understand God is working in the waiting. When you feel God is not moving fast enough, know your strength is the byproduct of the waiting and this is God's preparation period for you. Whatever you are expecting God to do, trust God to bring it to pass. In the interim, do not whine but wait on the Lord.

Set A Good Example

"In everything set them an example by doing what is good. In your teaching show integrity, seriousness and soundness of speech that cannot be condemned, so that those who oppose you may be ashamed because they have nothing bad to say about us."

— *Titus 2:7-8 (NIV)*

In my neighborhood, there was a lady who would curse from time to time. If she dropped a plate, she would curse. If she tripped and nearly fell, she would curse. She would only curse in certain situations.

One day, her 7-year-old daughter was in the kitchen helping her cook. The daughter mistakenly dropped a dish and you guessed it …the girl cursed! The mother was outraged and said, "What are you doing cursing? You know better than that!" Through tears in the little girl's voice; she looked up and said, "Momma, I just did what you would do — I cursed." The disappointment the little girl experienced was the result of following her mother's example.

An axiom that rings true is, "You may be the only Bible some people read and the only God some see." This axiom speaks to the importance of men and women of God handling situations in a godly fashion because someone is ALWAYS watching. When people are aware of the situation you are facing, their eyes/ears are fine-tuned to witness how you will handle it. Children watch you. Colleagues watch you. Strangers watch you. Classmates watch you. Other Christians watch you. May no one who observes your life be disappointed as a result of following your example.

Stop Trying, Start Trusting

"That day when evening came, he said to his disciples, 'Let us go over to the other side.' Leaving the crowd behind, they took him along, just as he was, in the boat. There were also other boats with him. A furious squall came up, and the waves broke over the boat, so that it was nearly swamped. Jesus was in the stern, sleeping on a cushion. The disciples woke him and said to him, 'Teacher, don't you care if we drown?' He got up, rebuked the wind and said to the waves, 'Quiet! Be still!' Then the wind died down and it was completely calm. He said to his disciples, 'Why are you so afraid? Do you still have no faith?'"

— Mark 4:35-40 (NIV)

Sometimes in life, the storms we face seem to overwhelm us. The storm seems unbearable, we have exhausted all resources and efforts trying to overcome. You have tried this, tried that, talked to this Pastor, talked to this minister, talked to this doctor, talked to that specialist, talked to this friend, talked to that relative, etc. Despite everything, the situation remains the same. Therefore, we find ourselves discouraged, isolated, hopeless and wanting to give up. Can you relate?

Often times, it is so easy to focus our attention on the ineffectiveness of our efforts that we forget about who is already IN us, on our ship. I imagine the disciples trying to handle the flood themselves using anything they could find. After their methods proved unsuccessful, they decided to try Jesus. In only a few words, Jesus calmed the sea. The disciples overlooked the power that existed within the ship. In your storm, do not forget Who is on your ship. Seek and rely on Him in your storm, rather than your own futile efforts. It is time to stop trying and start trusting. "Do you still have no faith?"

Repent and Restore

"… Repent! Turn away from all your offenses; then sin will not be your downfall. Rid yourselves of all the offenses you have committed, and get a new heart and a new spirit."

—Ezekiel 18:30-31 (NIV)

Have you ever done something outside of the will of God that made you feel like the scum of the earth? You do or say something you know was wrong in the eyes of God and you find yourself having a pity party. You feel like God should give up on you because it seems that you continually do things that are outside of His will. You feel, "Why should God continue to love me?" "God has to be tired of me and my mess," "I don't deserve to be deemed a man/woman of God," "I can't seem to get it together," and "I am always messing up."

God never expected perfection from His children! Because God is aware of our sinful tendencies, God generously provides us with grace and mercy. Based on our sinful actions, we sometimes feel like we deserve to die, deserve to have a disease, deserve to be imprisoned, or deserve to be in a negative situation. God's provision of grace and mercy gives us another chance (another chance, and another, and another — you get the picture) to learn from our mistakes.

Many great men and women of God in the Bible were guilty of doings things that displeased God. In many cases, they too, felt guilty and undeserving of God's love, but they learned from their sinful actions and restored their relationship with God. When we do or say things that displease God, the enemy's goal is to keep us focused on remaining in the sin rather than restoration of our godly relationship. Nevertheless, waddling in the sin and hosting a pity party does more harm than good. Though grace and mercy are not a license to sin, they drop the charges when sin occurs. When you fall to sin, get up, repent and get back in line with God. Repent and be restored!

Think Positive Thoughts

"Finally, brothers and sisters, whatever is true, whatever is noble, whatever is right, whatever is pure, whatever is lovely, whatever is admirable – if anything is excellent or praiseworthy –think about such things. "

— *Philippians 4:8 (NIV)*

Are you a person who always thinks the worst? In everything that happens, you think about the worst-case scenario. You almost feel as if you deserve nothing but negative outcomes, and you find it difficult to think in a positive light. "Why should this not happen?" "It's my fault, I deserve it," and "The odds are against me." Do you even *attempt* to think about the positive in situations or are you always consumed with the negative?

Different situations can flood the mind with a myriad of thoughts. Thoughts about employment, health, family situation, ministry, the economy, and many other things cross the mind. When you think about these things (and others), are your thoughts positive or negative?

Know this: Negativity is not of God! Negative thinking adversely affects you spiritually and physically; it can indicate a lack of faith and result in high blood pressure, nervous breakdowns, and other health risks. Ultimately, your mind and body will believe everything you tell it. Filling your mind with things that are noble, right, pure, lovely, admirable, excellent, or praiseworthy will position you to live the life of faith God has called us to live. Whatever the situation, think positive thoughts!

Take Advantage of the Opportunity

"Be wise in the way you act toward outsiders; make the most of every opportunity. Let your conversation be always full of grace, seasoned with salt, so that you may know how to answer everyone."

— Colossians 4:5-6 (NIV)

How often do we pass up the opportunity to share the gospel with people around us — family, friends, co-workers, or classmates? Because people look a certain way or because we *think* a certain way, we feel that they will not receive a Word from us. "Why would they listen to me when I used to drink with them?" "He/she practically raised me, why would they listen to me?" "He/she doesn't know me," or "This is not the right time/place." These are just a few of the excuses we relegated as reasons not to share the gospel with people around us. In addition to these excuses, we stereotype some people by the way they look, talk, or act. We have a tendency to make a self-determination as to whether a person will receive the Gospel message from us or not. However, this is not up to us, but up to the God within us. We are responsible for planting seeds and God determines the result (I Corinthians 3:6).

We are living in perilous times, so we must take advantage of every opportunity we have to share the gospel. There are people who have been deemed perpetually lost. Yet, God did not save us for us to sit back and disregard those considered outsiders. God cares about the outsiders, and we cannot forget we were once outsiders. In fact, there may be people who considered us perpetually lost. Nevertheless, someone took advantage of an opportunity to minister to us, so we should give *outsiders* the same opportunity. Webster's dictionary defines opportunity as *a* "good chance for advancement or progress." When we share the gospel with others, we are providing them with a *chance* for advancement from the world to the kingdom of God. Some people may not respond to the Gospel from us, but our responsibility is to plant, not to reap results. Paul spoke to this in I Corinthians 3:6: "I planted the seed, Apollos watered it, but God has been making it grow."

Detach from the Attachment

"... Let us throw off everything that hinders and the sin that so easily entangles. And let us run with perseverance the race that is marked out for us ..."

— *Hebrews 12:1 (NIV)*

During one fun-filled weekend, I participated in a three-legged race at my church. I was tied to another person to race against others who were tied together by one leg. When the coordinator said "go," my partner and I began to run. However, after a few strides, we both fell because neither of us was accustomed to being attached to someone else when trying to run. At the conclusion of the race, we laughed about how difficult it was to run successfully with someone else attached to you.

We sometimes attempt to run the race of life with people and things attached to us. Sometimes there comes a point in where you must to detach from attachments (people, places, and things) in order to successfully run the race God has set for you (and the people attached to you). No one can effectively run through the labyrinth of life with people, places, and things that are not purposed to be accompaniments. In your attempt to run with some attachments, you will discover yourself falling because in many ways you were created to run alone. The amazing thing about this is that sometimes God leads you to detach from something or someone that you wish to cling to. God sometimes leads you to detach from friends, family, and other people that you love and care about. In response to God's leading, we sometimes yell, "God, I don't want to let go!" It is undoubtedly difficult to detach from those you love, but it is imperative in order to fruitfully run the race of life. At this point in your life, detach from them, attach to Him, and go in the direction God is leading you to go.

Thank You, God

"... Give thanks in all circumstances; for this is God's will for you in Christ Jesus. "

— *I Thessalonians 5:18 (NIV)*

As a father, I am very intentional about teaching my children to say "thank you." As a way for them to develop the habit, I anticipate hearing the words whenever they are given something. One afternoon, I promised all three of them lollipops to enjoy after school. School ended and I was going to fulfill my promise to them. I gave the three of them lollipops but only one said thank you. As a result of only one child thanking me, I took them from the other two children. When I took the lollipops, they immediately erupted into tears because they missed out (only for a while) on what was promised to them. I took the lollipops from them because they acted ungrateful, and they quickly learned the importance of gratefulness and thanking their father.

When is the last time you told God thank you? Do you respond to God from a posture of entitlement or gratefulness? What's more, what if God removed from us that which He gives us simply because of our refusal to simply say "thank you." There is little that is worse than someone who is ungrateful. Alfred Painter said, "Saying thank you is more than good manners, it is good spirituality." Today, take a moment to thank God for what He has done or is doing in your life. Most times, we thank God for the material things we have, homes, cars, money, etc. However, we should also thank God for the intangibles — the ability to breathe, the activity of your limbs, a measure of health and strength, the ability to see and hear, and things one cannot quantify. In short, no matter the circumstances of our lives, there is always something to thank God for.

It's Just Favor!

"'The Lord has done this for me,' she said. 'In these days he has shown his favor and taken away my disgrace among the people.'"

— Luke 1:25 (NIV)

Have you ever received something you or others felt you did not deserve? You received a job you were not qualified for. You received a promotion over people who have more time and experience with the company. You were approved for a house or car loan with bad or subpar credit. There are countless things people receive and undeniably know only God could have provided. While great things are happening in the lives of some people, others are left wondering, "How did he/she do it?" "That isn't right," "That isn't fair," or "That didn't happen to or for me."

When it comes to the favor of God on your life, there is zero obligation to explain it to other people. Furthermore, it is incredibly difficult, if not impossible to explain miracles or happenings to others that even you cannot comprehend. Oftentimes, there is a sense of pressure to explain to jealous and curious people who try to figure out the miracles in your life. These covetous people attempt to understand how you received it and why they didn't, why you were approved and they weren't, why it happened for you and not them, and many other inquiries/curiosities. Ironically, and even comically, you have the same questions yourself. Therefore, the only answer you can give is, "I don't know how it happened, but it did. I know I don't deserve it; the only explanation I can give is — it's just favor!"

Just Do It

"My Father, if it is possible, may this cup be taken from me. Yet not as I will, but as you will."

— *Matthew 26:39 (NIV)*

In my childhood, my best friend and I lived around the corner from one another. One day, he and I decided to play basketball at his house. Before I left home, my mother gave me specific directions to do my chores prior to going to play ball. Well, I decided to do what I wanted to do by going to play ball then doing the chores later. After a short while at my friend's house, I received a call from my mother telling me to come home and do what I was told to do before I left. Needless to say, I was upset, but had to accept the reality that it was my fault.

Many times, God gives us specific instructions and we decide to do what we want to do and obey Him later. During this time, God sometimes sits back and allows us to do this for a while. However, after a while, God allows things to happen to bring us back *home* to do what we should have done in the beginning. God has to bring us back to the reality that He remains in control and as His children, we must do what He says. Of course, His timing is almost always opposite our timing, but His is most important. If there is something you are to do and you have postponed it until later, you have two options: 1) do it NOW 2) allow God to bring you back to reality and then you do it. Take it from me, option #2 is not a pleasant one. Just do it!

You Can Win With a Bad Hand

"Trust in the LORD with all your heart and lean not on your own understanding; in all your ways submit to him, and he will make your paths straight."

— *Proverbs 3:5-6 (NIV)*

While playing the card game of Spades, I was dealt a hand I was not too happy with. It seemed I had nothing to "win a book." When the cards were dealt and the game began, I looked over at my partner and said, "Man, I don't have a thing, all I can do is follow suit!" My focus went from trying to win books to just going along with whatever card was played. If someone played a diamond, I played a diamond. If someone played a club, I played a club. You get the picture - I just followed suit.

Many times in life we face some situations and circumstances that we do not understand. You don't know or understand why things are the way they are. You look at your "hand" (your resources) and determine that you don't have a thing. When you consider your past, you feel you are at a disadvantage. When you contemplate your lack of experience, you can become deflated and not pursue what you desire to pursue. Nevertheless, it is at this point one must make a decision to follow suit. We follow suit by trusting God to handle situations in His way and in His timing. One must not rely on self to overcome situations (books), but trust God and follow suit. If you follow suit, you will discover that with God, you can win with a bad hand.

Talk To Him

"'...In my distress I called to the LORD, and he answered me. From deep in the realm of the dead I called for help, and you listened to my cry.'"

—Jonah 2:2 (NIV)

Have you ever felt like God was tired of talking to you about the same issues? You say to yourself, "I know God is tired of me talking to Him about this, I know I am probably getting on His nerves." I have said this many times regarding some issues in my life. One day in my quiet time I said, "God, don't I get on your nerves talking to you about the same stuff all the time, day after day, sometimes minute after minute?" His response was, "I would rather you talk to Me about the same things than you not talk to Me at all. At least you are talking to Me."

We must realize that God never gets tired or frustrated when we talk to Him — even about the same things. He longs to talk to us and He is always there to listen. When in distress, we often seek people's good advice, rather than God's divine assistance. We seek people's opinions to patch the situation, rather than God who can heal it. There may be something in your life that you feel God is tired of talking about, but know that He never gets tired. He is always waiting and willing to talk to you. Talk to Him!

You Don't Have To Be Strong

"Jesus wept."

—*John 11:35 (NIV)*

Are you someone who always feels that you have to be the strong one in a particular situation? Do you believe that if you aren't strong, everything and everyone will fall apart? When the family experiences tragedy, do you feel the need to be strong for everyone else? No matter what happens with you or your family, it is you who has to be strong? Everyone looks to you. You are the strong Christian in the family. You are the backbone. Are you invincible in that you do not experience hurt or pain? If you are human, you can and will hurt.

Many people are experiencing the pain of losing loved ones. Family members are being deployed to Iraq, you're watching children make wrong decisions in life, etc. The list goes on and on about the many painful situations that arise in life. Many feel the need to be the "strong one." The fact that Jesus actually shed tears in the Bible sticks out in my mind. The Man who would feel the most like the 'strong One' was the One who cried. Jesus felt the pain of losing a loved one to the point where it brought tears. Jesus sets an example for us. He did not do what some of us do - "hold them (tears) back" to be strong for Mary and Martha. Someone needs to know that you cannot be strong all the time! If Jesus felt pain to the point of tears, you can rest assured knowing that you will too — now or later. However, when these situations arise in life, be reminded that you don't have to be "strong;" it is okay to cry. Jesus did!

Break the Routine

"Therefore let all the faithful pray to you while you may be found; surely the rising of the mighty waters will not reach him."

— *Psalm 32:6 (NIV)*

"By day the LORD directs his love, at night his song is with me - a prayer to the God of my life."

— *Psalm 42:8 (NIV)*

When a friend of mine purchased a newly released CD, every day she would listen to the same songs, at the same time, at the same place. She had developed a routine for listening to the CD. However, after months of this routine, the CD began to get "old" to her. The same CD she used to enjoy, she later found it difficult to even listen to it. There came a point in which she felt there was a need for change, so she began to look for a new CD to renew her excitement. Needless to say, that CD got old too. To solve this issue, my friend decided to break the routine and listen to different things, at different times, in different places.

In quiet times with God, many people have established a routine. Some pray at the same time, same place, and about the same things. After a while, one can find it difficult to get excited about spending quiet time with God. The quiet time that was once exciting and enjoyable has become old and boring. We do not serve a boring God and we should periodically break the normal routine of our time spent with Him. Praying in a different place, listening, instead of talking during prayer, or reading a different passage, are just a few ways the routine can be broken. Lately, if you find it difficult to bring yourself to spend time with God, it may be an indicator that you need to break the routine.

Free Yourself

"If we confess our sins, he is faithful and just and will forgive us our sins and purify us from all unrighteousness."

— *1 John 1:9 (NIV)*

Imagine this: There was a young man who committed a crime and was put in jail. When he admits to the judge his wrongdoing, the judge pardons him and hands him the keys to his cell. The young man leaves the presence of the judge to return to his cell. Rather than leaving the jail cell and returning to his home, he decided to stay in jail because he felt like the judge was too lenient on him. Therefore, we have a young man with the keys to freedom in his hands, but he decides to remain in prison.

Many times you can commit sin and issue yourself a "self-sentence." You feel you deserve the worst sentence possible, so that is what you issue to yourself. You punish yourself by taking away things you enjoy simply because this is a part of your "self-sentence." However, when you make a "true confession" to God, your sin is pardoned and it is up to you to be freed from your "self-imprisonment." Many times God forgives you of your sins only for you to return to a life under the "self-sentence." How long will you keep yourself handcuffed? How long will you keep yourself shackled? How long will you stay "locked up" in the house? God forgives ALL sins. However, you must forgive yourself. "Then neither do I condemn you," Jesus declared. "Go now and leave your life of sin" (John 8:11). Free yourself!

This is Just a Commercial

"...weeping may stay for the night, but rejoicing comes in the morning."

— Psalm 30:5 (NIV)

Have you ever been watching your favorite TV show or soap opera and a commercial comes on at the most inopportune time? The show is "getting good" and you cannot wait to see what is going to happen next. You sit in anticipation and... commercial break! You sit there and you say, "The show was getting good and a commercial came on, I hate commercials!" The commercials are playing and you are saying, "These commercials need to hurry up so I can get back to my show." Finally, the commercials end and the show resumes. However, in order to get back to the show, you had to watch the commercials.

It is during those moments when everything seems to be going well, that a storm comes at what we consider to be the most inopportune time. It seemed like your life was getting better and better as the days passed by. You were in great expectation of what good would happen next and BOOM ... a storm! You sit there and you say, "My life was going fine and then this storm comes, I don't like storms, I wish it would hurry up and pass by." In the show of life, there are some commercials (storms) that we have to experience. Just as commercials are a part of TV, storms are a part of life. However, it is great to know that the commercials don't last as long as the show. You may be in a storm, just remember that "It's just a commercial, it won't last long."

Deal with the Small Things

"Be alert and of sober mind. Your enemy the devil prowls around like a roaring lion looking for someone to devour."

— 1 Peter 5:8 (NIV)

Many homeowners go over and beyond to protect their homes from termites. Termites are very small creatures that invade people's residences and literally "eat them out of a house and a home." When one termite enters the home, many others follow. As the quantity of these small creatures increases, the damage to the home also increases. These small things can destroy big things, if too many accumulate. Therefore, it is important to homeowners to have their homes protected against the invasion of termites.

It is important that we protect our minds from the termites of life - small things that invade the mind and cause harm. We must go over and beyond to recognize that situations we determine to be "small things" can cause tremendous harm if they are not dealt with. When people say, "That's small, you can get past that," "You can't let stuff like that get to you," or "How important is that?" those are the things that can cause harm if allowed to accumulate. We must recognize that the devil uses what we (and others) determine to be "small things" to destroy ministries, relationships and other areas of life. Know that "small things" destroy "big things," therefore, you must deal with the "small things" before they become "big things."

Actions Speak Louder Than Words

"Jesus replied, "Anyone who loves me will obey my teaching. My Father will love them, and we will come to them and make our home with them. Anyone who does not love me will not obey my teaching. These words you hear are not my own; they belong to the Father who sent me."

—John 14:23-24 (NIV)

I have learned throughout life that actions speak louder than words. If you say you love a person with your mouth, it is more important to demonstrate your love by your actions. If you say you will do something, it is more important that you do what you said you would do. If you say you will not do something, it is important that you not do what you said you would not do. However, there are many areas of life in which you are held accountable to be a person of your word.

What if God held us accountable to be a person of our word? We say we love Him, but do we demonstrate in our daily life that we love Him? It is easy to say we love Him, but in what ways is that love shown? Do we do what God asks of us, instead of just "saying" what we will do? Do we not do what God asks us not to do, or do we "say" we will not do it? Do our daily actions match up with the words we say? This can be applied to life at home, workplace, church, or other areas. Just remember actions always speak louder than words.

101

Wear Your Seatbelt

"Rejoice always, pray continually, give thanks in all circumstances; for this is God's will for you in Christ Jesus."

— *I Thessalonians 5:16-18 (NIV)*

A seatbelt should be worn for protection just in case an accident occurs. Of course, one never knows when, where, or how an accident will occur, however, one should wear a seatbelt to ensure protection. Not wearing a seatbelt subjects a person to extreme injuries in the event of an accident. Therefore, I join the federal government in recommending the wearing of seatbelts. Simply wearing the seatbelt has saved many lives.

In life, we never know when, where, or how tests or attacks of the enemy will come. However, prayer serves as the seatbelt to protect us at all times. Prayer protects us from the injuries of sin, depression, anger, and many others. Not maintaining a regular prayer life subjects us to many things and provides the enemy a direct path to make us fall victim to injuries. Therefore, I join with Paul in recommending that we "pray continually." Simply wearing the seatbelt of prayer has conquered many situations. Wear your seatbelt — at all times!

Beggars Can't Be Choosy

"But the fruit of the Spirit is love, joy, peace, forbearance, kindness, goodness, faithfulness, gentleness and self-control. Against such things there is no law."

— *Galatians 5:22-23 (NIV)*

A woman goes into the grocery store and she has a taste for grapes. She goes to the produce section and finds the grapes she likes most. Although she is craving grapes, she only wants a few. Therefore, she takes about three or four grapes from the bushel and takes them to the cashier for checkout. Needless to say, the cashier looks at her in amazement and says, "Ma'am, you cannot only purchase three or four grapes, you have to purchase the whole bushel." The woman replies, "I don't want that many, I only want three or four." The cashier then says, "Ma'am I understand that, but you still have to purchase the entire bushel." The woman finally purchases the bushel of grapes even though she does not want all of the grapes.

When it comes to the fruit of the spirit, many of us have the attitude of the woman in this fictional story. We have a "taste" or desire only for a few things listed in the text. Many crave peace, but do not wish to demonstrate the kindness. Many desire joy, but do not want the faithfulness. The list could go on and on about which of the virtues we might pick from the list. However, one must notice there is no "-s" on the word fruit in the text to make it plural. Therefore, in order for us to obtain the fruit of the Spirit, we strive for the whole "bushel," which consists of love, joy, peace, patience, kindness, goodness, faithfulness, gentleness and self-control.

It's in the Package

"I press on toward the goal to win the prize for which God has called me heavenward in Christ Jesus."

— *Philippians 3:14 (NIV)*

My friends and I are big fans of the Eclipse immediate breath control gum. The outside of the package lists four things to encourage you to buy the gum: 1) quick burst of freshening, lasts and lasts 2) sugar-free, does not promote tooth decay 3) each piece sealed for superior freshness 4) perforated package fits pocket or purse.

Many times we want an immediate blessing that lasts and lasts. However, if God always blessed us quickly, it would promote spiritual decay because we would begin to focus on ourselves and live God-free lives. It is important that God has some fresh blessings for each of us, however, we may have to press through in order to obtain them. Each piece of gum is under foil that must be pressed through in order to get to it. In life, there will be times when you have to press through some difficult times, heartache and pain, but the blessing is in the package. God is so mighty; He blesses each of us in a way that "fits" our individual lives. Keep pressing, your blessing is in the package!

Focus On Your Own Basket

"I know what it is to be in need, and I know what it is to have plenty. I have learned the secret of being content in any and every situation, whether well fed or hungry, whether living in plenty or in want. I can do all this through him who gives me strength."

— Philippians 4:12-13 (NIV)

Have you ever been in the grocery store and noticed other shoppers looking at what you have in your basket? You have in your basket the things that you came for or the things that came across that were good deals. It seems that the other shoppers should be focusing on their own list, but somehow they are consumed with what you have. Some are paying so much attention that they will even ask you, "Where did you find this or that?" You want to say, "Why are you looking in my basket? Focus on your own!"

As children of God, it is important that we are focused on what God is doing in our lives and not focus our attention on what He is doing in the lives of others. Sometimes we can put so much attention on others that we become covetous and jealous of them while overlooking the things that God wants to reveal or place in our lives. We become consumed with she can do this, he has that, she has this gift, he is good at that, etc. So what if others have graduated, others have a better job, others are married, or any other thing you can think of? God is saying, "Why are you looking at their basket (life)? Focus on your own." The same things you see in their baskets are the same things you can have. However, you may miss or overlook them because you refuse to focus on your own basket.

There is a King in Your Corner

"Be strong and courageous. Do not be afraid or terrified because of them, for the Lord your God goes with you; he will never leave you nor forsake you."

— Deuteronomy 31:6 (NIV)

Cracker Barrel is one of my family's favorite restaurants. Because others enjoy it as well, we would often have to be placed on a waiting list before being seated. After putting our name on the list, my wife and I would often play checkers while we waited. One day, my wife was beating me badly, she had the majority of my chips. Though she had the majority of my chips, at some point in the game I managed to get a king. If you know anything about checkers, you know the king can make moves ordinary chips cannot make.

As our game continued and my wife continued to get the best of me, I reached a point where all I had on the board was a king. Having only a king, I had to make the best of the situation. When she made a move, I simply moved my king to the corner because a king in the corner cannot be jumped. When she made another move, I moved my king to the other corner. This went on for a few minutes until she said, "Tim, you may as well give up because I have all of your chips." I looked at her and said, "Baby, you got all of my chips, but as long my king is in the corner, I'm still in the game."

Have you ever felt like the enemy has all of your chips? Points in life when it seems you take two steps forward and five steps back? Points when it seems all of your efforts prove empty and futile? Absolutely, huh? Even now, you may feel abandoned, depressed or despondent, but be encouraged that as long as God is in your corner, you are still in the game. It does not matter what is taking place in your life, it does not matter what you have done, if you are a child of God, the King is in our corner … you are still in the game!

Live What You Look

"Do not merely listen to the word, and so deceive yourselves. Do what it says. Anyone who listens to the word but does not do what it says is like someone who looks at his face in a mirror and, after looking at himself, goes away and immediately forgets what he looks like. But whoever looks intently into the perfect law that gives freedom, and continues in it — not forgetting what they have heard, but doing it — they will be blessed in what they do."

—James 1:22-25 (NIV)

It is no secret that I love playing basketball. In fact, although I turn 41 tomorrow, playing basketball is still an integral part of my weekly exercise regimen. While I enjoy playing basketball, I absolutely hate to lose. I hate losing, so when I have opportunity to pick my teammates, I choose them very carefully. However, there are times when you have to pick people whom you have never met and have no knowledge of their skill (or lack thereof) on the court. It is always interesting with some guys. They walk in adorned with matching shorts and shirts, some of them wear the arm or leg sleeve that some of the NBA guys wear, they have on stylish socks, and of course some nice shoes. When you talk to them, they quickly rattle off the history and records of their favorite teams and players. Looking at them and listening to them would lead you to believe they have great skills playing ball. However, when they get on the court... they can't play a lick. If their lives depend on them making a shot, they need to make funeral arrangements. Their look and level of basketball knowledge is great, but on the court they are not living out what they appeared to be.

When I thought about this, I quickly realized the same thing happens in church among believers. There are people who look the part, know some gospel songs, know some Bible verses, but when they get on the court of life, they are found to have great knowledge of God, but are not living for God. These are people who can be described as being *in church*, but the church has not made its way into them. Shame on us if we are in church week after week, singing/serving/sitting regularly, listening to sermons week after week, but are not living out who we appear or profess to be both individually, or corporately, as a church. As a Christian or as a church, we cannot be people who transmit hope (where we give the impression of God) but have not been transformed by hope to the degree that we transport hope (where we make an impact for God). Let us live what we look.

God Will Get You Out

"For no word from God will ever fail."

— *Luke 1:37 (NIV)*

"Look to the Lord and his strength; seek his face always."

— *I Chronicles 16:11 (NIV)*

One day, my son Timothy was playing with some kids at a local community center when somehow his leg got stuck between the seats on a bench. The kids he was playing with were trying to get him free but were unsuccessful. A member of the church alongside one of the deacons were trying to free him but were unsuccessful. It seemed no one could free him from the situation he was stuck in. He was stuck, really stuck. One of the kids ran to me exclaiming, "Your son is stuck and nobody can get him out!" I walked down the hall and slid him out of the place He was stuck in.

You see, he was in a position that appeared to have him stuck. He was crying, he was in pain, but His father was not only present but had the power to get him free. There are points in life where you can feel stuck and nothing and no one can seem to free you. Books, friends, Google and whatever else all prove to be impotent in getting you out of the place you are stuck in. Nevertheless, sometimes God places us in a position that only God can get us out of. While this fact can be discouraging because of the uncertainty of when God will free you, the good news is that there is no place that God is not in and that He cannot get you out of. God is bigger than your problems and wider than your wilderness. No matter the circumstance or situation, be encouraged today that God can and will get you out.

From Scratch

"He is the Rock, his works are perfect, and all his ways are just. A faithful God who does no wrong, upright and just is he."

— *Deuteronomy 32:4 (NIV)*

Throughout the years, there have been many advances in the food industry. Nowadays, it seems almost anything can be cooked within minutes. Microwave dinners, frozen pizzas, instant coffee, just-add-water pancakes, and many other things can be prepared with minimal time. However, there are some old-school people who specialize in making things from scratch. It is amazing the difference in tastes between that which is processed and what is made from scratch. When dishes are made from scratch, various individual ingredients are mixed together to create a particular dish. Making a dish from scratch takes more time and effort, but tastes exponentially better than what comes from the microwave.

This is how God works with and operates with us. Many times, because we live in such an instant society, we want things now, we want answers to our prayers now, we want them to come to fruition soon after they depart from our lips. However, we cannot allow the microwave syndrome of the world to filter into our Christian lives. God is not a God that answers prayers instantaneously. For us, it seems as if our waiting is wasting, but for God waiting is working. We serve a God of excellence and He specializes in making things from scratch. God takes the necessary time and effort that He needs to create what is PERFECT for us. We must understand that God takes various things, situations, and

112

experiences from our lives and mixes them together to craft what He desires for us to have or for us to be. Whenever we are getting impatient, whenever we reach a point where we question if God is going to come through, know God is not a microwave. What God is doing in your life, God is doing from scratch.

Betcha See a Blessing

"... I have come that they may have life, and have it to the full."

—*John 10:10 (NIV)*

Most people who know me have found me to be a big fan of Chips Ahoy cookies. I love eating those cookies! The tagline for the cookies is "Betcha bite a chip." This is to imply that every time you bite into a Chips Ahoy cookie, you will more than likely bite into a chocolate chip. No matter how small of a bite you take, you are guaranteed to bite a chocolate chip because so many are in each cookie. Throughout the years of eating Chips Ahoy cookies, I have found the tagline to be pretty accurate. The chips of chocolate may be small, but they are everywhere in the cookie. Betcha bite a chip!

When each of us looks at our lives, we see the blessings of God in every area of our lives. You may not like your job, but you have one. You may not have a job, but you are not on the streets. You may not have the clothes or shoes you want, but you have clothes and shoes to wear. You may be sick, but you are still alive. You may not have as much money as you would like, but you are not totally broke. The list can go on and on about the blessings all of us have. No matter how one may try to deny or ignore God's presence and blessings in their lives, one is guaranteed to see His blessings present everywhere. Betcha see a blessing!

No Turn Signal

*"The Almighty is beyond our reach and exalted in power;
in his justice and great righteousness, he does not oppress."*

—*Job 37:23 (NIV)*

One day while driving my vehicle, a car pulled over in front of me without activating the turn signal. I was upset because he unexpectedly turned in front of me. I felt disrespected because in my opinion, he should have given me a signal to let me know he wanted to get in my lane. If he would have given me a signal, more than likely I would have felt better about letting him over. However, it is still possible that I would have been a bit irritated if I allowed him in my lane and he didn't drive like I thought he should.

There are times in our lives in which God does things without providing a signal of what He is about to do. We sometimes get upset because He allows things to happen when we least expect them. We get upset because we feel God could have at least provided a signal, then it would be much easier to accept. However, just as drivers pull over into our lanes without notice, we must recognize God's sovereignty to do the same in our lives. Even if God provides a signal for what He is about to do, we can still find ourselves irritated because things are not going the way we feel they should. As difficult as it is to do, we must be willing to allow God to drive our lives and accept when He makes turns without using a signal.

Let It Pass

"Yes, my soul, find rest in God; my hope comes from him. Truly he is my rock and my salvation; he is my fortress, I will not be shaken. My salvation and my honor depend on God; he is my mighty rock, my refuge. Trust in him at all times, you people; pour out your hearts to him, for God is our refuge."

— Psalm 62:5-8 (NIV)

After arriving at the airport on a business trip, I headed outside to wait for the bus to transport me to the hotel. As I waited, there were several buses to come by, some of them even looked like the bus I was supposed to be on. They were nice and shiny, and sometimes pulled aside to extend the invitation for me to come aboard. Though they looked nice and extended opportunities, though the weather was brisk, I let them pass by because they could not get me where I needed to go.

Everything and everyone that comes to you is not for you. They may look good, they may even resemble what you desire, but let them pass by. In fact, you may even be in the cold of life, but have the courage to let them pass by. The opportunities extended to you may seem ideal, but sometimes what is good may not be God. Despite what the person or situation appears to be, they are unable to get you where you are purposed to be.

One For All, All For One

"... If my people, who are called by my name, will humble themselves and pray and seek my face and turn from their wicked ways, then will I hear from heaven and will forgive their sin and will heal their land."

— *II Chronicles 7:14 (NIV)*

One morning on garbage pickup day, I noticed a pack of dogs that were gathered together walking through the neighborhood looking for trash to get into. There were various breeds of dogs gathered on one accord with one common goal. When they found something to get into, they all were involved with the same garbage can. What was amazing is that none of them were fighting with one another, but they all worked together and enjoyed the fruit of their labor together.

As much as we may not desire dogs getting into our trash and littering the neighborhood, the dogs modeled a camaraderie that Christians should take heed to. Despite denominational differences, if we believe Jesus is the Son of God, we should all gather together on one accord with a common goal — to edify the body of Christ. Nevertheless, we often get sidetracked and allow differences to hinder us from achieving the things God wants to achieve. We ALL love God, we ALL want to live in His will, and we ALL want to please Him with our lives. Therefore, it is important that we ALL work together and we ALL enjoy the fruit of our labor together. One purpose for all Christians, all Christians for one God. One for all and all for one!

Catch Spills Early

"'In your anger do not sin.' Do not let the sun go down while you are still angry, and do not give the devil a foothold."

— Ephesians 4:26-27 (NIV)

While eating lunch with co-workers, I spilled ketchup on my shirt. The right thing to do would have been to wash it or have it cleaned as soon as possible. However, I changed clothes and did not deal with the spill on the shirt. The next time I wanted to wear the shirt, I found that what started out to be a small spill had become a stain. I took the shirt to the cleaners only to be told that the stain could not be removed and that I should have dealt with it soon after the spill. Because I neglected to do that, I could no longer wear the shirt without the stain being evident.

People in your life may have *spilled* on you by hurting you in some shape, form or fashion. There was something said or done that really hurt you. However, when this happens, there is a tendency to change clothes by pushing it to the back of your mind and not dealing with the hurt soon after the occurrence. Therefore, the next time you see the person, you may even be reminded of how they hurt you and you find that the anger that was once a spill is forming a stain. You have been stained when you find yourself at a point of no return, forgiveness is far from your mind, and you cannot move beyond it. When people hurt you, it is important that you deal with it by talking about how they hurt you. Keeping it inside will cause it to fester and promote years of anger and resentment toward them. When people hurt you, catch spills early!

Believe God, Not Them

"The person without the Spirit does not accept the things that come from the Spirit of God but considers them foolishness, and cannot understand them because they are discerned only through the Spirit."

— *I Corinthians 2:14 (NIV)*

Over the past few years, I have spoken to many people who have a divine purpose in life, but are preoccupied with the thoughts and opinions of other people. "How do I deal with the people who know my past?" "Will they believe me?" and "They will say that I am not 'for real.'" The list goes on about the many statements that are made by people who are hindered by the opinions and thoughts of other people. So what does a person who struggles with these hindrances do?

It is important you realize that not everyone will understand, believe, or accept God's call on your life. However, the call on your life is for YOU to believe, not them. No one believed Mary was pregnant by the Holy Spirit to birth the Son of God, but SHE believed and gave birth. No one believed Sarah could conceive at the age of 90, but SHE believed and gave birth. Neither would have accomplished these things if they focused on the thoughts and opinions of others. You, too, are pregnant with a purpose, you cannot allow people to determine your destiny, and cause you to abort what God has placed in you. People may not and will not believe, but you must believe Him, not them!

You Must Shed

"If anyone comes to me and does not hate father and mother, wife and children, brothers and sisters - yes, even his own life - he cannot be my disciple."

— Luke 14:26 (NIV)

As an adolescent, I was simultaneously fearful of and fascinated by snakes. Although I never desired to own one as a pet, the various kinds of snakes and their way of life was amazing to me. What was most amazing about snakes was the fact that they shed their skin several times throughout their lives. The reason why snakes shed skin is because snakes grow continuously during their lifetime, but the skin does not grow with them. Therefore, as the snake grows, it becomes imperative that it sheds the old skin and allows new skin to come forth.

As children of God, we should continuously be growing to higher levels during our lifetimes. Just as the snake's skin serves its purpose and is shed, there are some people in life that are there to serve a purpose, but must be shed after the purpose has been completed. Are they bad people? No! Are you better than they are? No! However, a snake cannot grow to 15 feet and expect to live in 10 feet of skin. The snake may love, enjoy, and want to keep the skin it has at 10 feet, but it must shed it as it grows. There may be people that you love, enjoy, and want to keep, but their purpose has been completed. As you continue to grow, although painful and difficult to do, you must shed!

Functional or Dysfunctional?

"... But whose delight is in the law of the LORD, and who meditates on his law day and night."

— *Psalm 1:2 (NIV)*

There are many cell phone companies all over the country. In my area, there is a company that is very popular because of their cheap prices and calling plans. However, the company does not have as many towers as some of the larger companies, which results in reception problems. Nevertheless, many people purchase the cell phones as they do not want to sacrifice the money for one of better quality. The phones function well, however, it is difficult for the phone to receive a signal in the rain, thereby making the phone dysfunctional. However, a better-quality phone would be functional in all circumstances.

Some people are content with their current relationship with God. Some have confessed Jesus Christ as their personal Savior, attend church every Sunday, and profess to being strong Christians. Great! However, these are people who attend church regularly, but spend no personal time with God. These people do not have the spiritual towers that others who are involved have. Therefore, when the rainy days of life come, it can be difficult to receive a signal (Word) from God. As a result, they become dysfunctional in the storms of life. By sacrificing personal time in favor of spending time with God, one will develop a better relationship with God and be functional in all circumstances. Today, be sure to choose the functional over the dysfunctional.

Seek Refuge

"The LORD is a refuge for the oppressed, a stronghold in times of trouble."

— Psalm 9:9 (NIV)

Can you imagine a person standing outside his home on a cold and rainy day? It is thundering and lightning and the person is standing there cold, wet, and with no umbrella. This person decides to stand out in the rain and wait for it to stop. Of course, one would like to ask the person, "Why don't you go in the house until the storm clears?" After hearing the question, the person realizes he is in front of his own home and that standing out in the rain makes no sense, so he decides to go inside.

The story above is fictional and may seem weird, but it holds true for many of us. Many of us stand in the midst of trouble waiting on the trouble to cease. Many stand in the midst of storms waiting for the storms to cease. We are like the person in the story, standing in the midst of the storm trying to figure things out rather than coming into the house. Often times, we forget that we have a Father in whom we can take refuge to hold and keep us when we are in trouble or until the storm passes. Whatever your storm or trouble may be, do not spend time trying to figure things out or trying to come up with a solution. Instead, seek refuge in God and know that this too shall pass.

Do It In the Game

"Rise up; this matter is in your hands...so take courage and do it."

—Ezra 10:4 (NIV)

During warm-ups before a basketball game, my team and I were doing lay-ups to loosen up. During lay-ups, some guys enjoyed dunking the ball to loosen up or to simply show off. One-handed dunks, two-handed dunks and backward dunks are just a few of the types done during warm-ups, and they look good, but they do not count. After a few dunks, my friend pulled me to the side and said, "You have the ability to dunk, but dunking during warm-ups is no good to us, you need to dunk in the game."

In the game of life, many people are very knowledgeable about the Word. We know what we should do when we face a particular situation. "I will do this, I will do that, I will say this or I will say that," are just a few statements we make during "warm-ups." Everything sounds and feels good coming out of the mouth, but it does not count because we are not in the actual situation. We can even give advice to others when they face certain situations. It is one thing to have the knowledge of what to do in certain situations, but doing what you know is most important. Do it in the game!

It's Not in Walking Distance

"... Faith by itself, if it is not accompanied by action, is dead."

—James 2:17 (NIV)

While in college, the basic things I needed were available in places that were in walking distance. Snacks, laundry detergent, and small restaurants could all be found in walking distance. However, when I wanted to step it up a bit, those places were not within walking distance. The nice restaurants, music stores and shopping malls were not within walking distance. Therefore, in order to get to the greater places, I had to put forth extra effort to get to them. The task was difficult without a car. However, when I got there, it was well worth it.

As Christians, we often want things to come easily. There are many things that we would like to see, do, or be done. However, we sometimes fail to put forth the effort necessary to accomplish those things. We want the prize but don't want to go through the process to get it. We want it to be in walking distance, without much effort. Thoughts and ideas are no good without action. When we think of what it takes to pursue our dreams, we give up because we want things to be within walking distance. Although extra effort is required, know there are greater things in store for us in places that may not be within walking distance. It is time to act on what we have thought about for weeks, months, or maybe even years! That which we dream of will come to pass only when action is put forth and we realize that it's not in walking distance.

Sprinkle It On Everything

"But seek first his kingdom and his righteousness, and all these things will be given to you as well."

— *Matthew 6:33 (NIV)*

"Do not be anxious about anything, but in every situation, by prayer and petition, with thanksgiving, present your requests to God."

— *Philippians 4:6 (NIV)*

Periodically, the young adult males have "Fellas Night Out" in which we all get together and talk about various issues. One night, we chose to have fellowship at a local restaurant. As soon as the food arrived, one guy immediately began sprinkling salt and pepper on all his food. After a few seconds of watching this, I asked "Why are you putting salt and pepper on everything and you haven't even tasted it? The food may be seasoned well enough where you may not need it." He simply replied, "No matter what I eat or how well seasoned the food is, in my eyes everything needs a little salt and pepper."

In life, there are many decisions to be made. Relationship decisions. Job decisions. Family decisions. Leadership decisions. Many other decisions can be added to the list. However, it is important that no matter how good (well-seasoned) something or someone seems to be, we should be mindful to sprinkle prayer on the decision BEFORE we make it. Often times, it seems that the best decision is obvious, so we make the decision then pray about it afterwards. There is always a possibility that we could be wrong about what seems to obviously be a good decision, so everything could use a little prayer and meditation before making it. Sprinkle prayer on everything? YES!

From Crawling to Walking

"Then he said to them all: Whoever wants to be my disciple must deny themselves and take up their cross daily and follow me. For whoever wants to save their life will lose it, but whoever loses their life for me will save it."

— *Luke 9:23-24 (NIV)*

One day I spoke with a friend from high school after a while of not communicating. After we caught one another up on our lives, I asked her about her son. She began to explain how excited she was about watching him walk. She went on and on about how she had become accustomed to watching him crawl and it was exciting to see him finally walk. Every parent I know has been excited to see his or her child move from crawling to walking.

In this Christian walk, you can find yourself crawling slowly through or in situations. Many times, we know EXACTLY what God wants us to do, but we are slow to move (crawl). When God prompts us to move away from a person or situation, we crawl around in the situation and never walk out of it. Sometimes we are even able to give advice to others who may be experiencing the same situation, however, we crawl even while we encourage them to walk! There may be a situation that you are crawling around in and you KNOW God wants you to walk out. The Parent is waiting with great anticipation to watch you move from crawling to walking!

It Hurts So Good

"Blessed are you when people insult you, persecute you and falsely say all kinds of evil against you because of me. Rejoice and be glad, because great is your reward in heaven, for in the same way they persecuted the prophets who were before you."

— *Matthew 5:11-12 (NIV)*

There was a young man who joined a health club after months of not exercising. In one workout, he lifted weights to tone his muscles. In another workout, he performed cardiovascular exercises to build his endurance. After a week of workouts, the young man was sore and complained to his trainer. The trainer advised him that the fact he was sore was a good thing and it was simply an indicator that he was working muscles that had not been used previously. He assured the young man that he was becoming stronger. The trainer told him to say to himself, "It hurts so good," when he feels the pain of his workouts.

You may be experiencing persecutions you have never experienced before. These persecutions are painful because you are doing all you can to live a godly life and you do not understand why the persecutions hurt so badly. The persecutions are from people you never thought would hurt you or for reasons that are ridiculous! The Bible advises us that persecutions will come, and though not pleasant to experience, we should rejoice. Therefore, the next time you begin to feel down and discouraged about your persecutions, know that God is exercising your faith to become stronger. Remember that the temporary pain of today, will make you stronger tomorrow. Keep reminding yourself, "It hurts so good."

Put It On the Belt

"Cast all your anxiety on Him because he cares for you."

— I Peter 5:7 (NIV)

On a recent business trip, I was in the baggage claim area waiting for my bags. As I waited, I began to reflect on how the bags ultimately get to me. After the plane is unloaded, there are employees who take each piece of luggage and place it on the belt to be picked up by someone. There are small bags, medium bags, and/or large bags, but they ALL go on the same belt. The employees have no idea who the bags belong to; their job is simply to empty the aircraft of all luggage and place them on the belt to be retrieved at the end of the belt.

In life, there are some things we need to throw on God. We spend time trying to figure out how this will be done, how will this be accomplished, wondering if it is too late, what will happen, etc. We have many questions (pieces of luggage) we have been carrying around for weeks, months, or maybe even years. God says, "Your job is not to question; your job is to put everything on the belt and know that I am at the end to retrieve them." Whether your cares or situations are small, medium, or large (in your eyes), they ALL go to the same One, just place them on the belt!

Roll With It

"Forget the former things; do not dwell on the past. See, I am doing a new thing! Now it springs up; do you not perceive it? I am making a way in the wilderness and streams in the wasteland."

— *Isaiah 43:18-19 (NIV)*

Have you ever met someone who finds it difficult to adapt to change? They are accustomed to things being done a certain way. If something is not done a certain way, it is wrong. There are some people who refuse to change neighborhoods, jobs, schools, clothing styles, cars, and other situations. These people are used to things the way they are and do not want them to change - EVER! It is not that the change is wrong, but it is simply not what they are used to. In today's society, there are many things that have changed and we may not like it, however, we have to roll with it.

In the church, there are many people who find it difficult to adapt to changes in today's society. Church buildings have changed. The order of worship has changed. Worship has changed. Music has changed. Praise has changed. A lot has changed over the years and it is important that we adapt to the changes. God is reaching people through praise dancing, contemporary music, Christian rap and other things that are non-traditional. It is not that the changes are wrong, but they are what some are not used to. God's objective is for people to be saved. He never gave a particular method. If the message is intact, do not become swayed by the method. God is doing a new thing and we simply need to roll with it!

Thank God For Grace

"But by the grace of God I am what I am, and his grace to me was not without effect."

- I Corinthians 15:10 (NIV)

Have you ever wondered how you made it through a situation? You never imagined being able to get over the relationship that did not work. You never thought you could function without a job. You never thought you would have peace of mind. You never thought you could pass the class. There are many things that we never thought we could do, but God saw us through.

Contrary to popular belief, who you are and who you have become is not because of you, it is merely because of the grace of God. None of us deserve anything, but by the grace of God, He saw fit to bless us. Often times, we can get caught up in the *I, me, my,* and *mine* syndrome. However, when we think of all we have gone through and where God has brought us, it leads us to the *He, His,* and *Him* syndrome. He brought you out of the situation. His love saved your life. It is because of God that you have peace that surpasses all understanding. Today, take a moment to remind yourself that you are who you are because of His grace. Thank God for His grace!

Ride the Bench

"The LORD will fight for you; you need only to be still."

— Exodus 14:14 (NIV)

Most sports teams are comprised of both star players and those who, most times, do not play or ride the bench. In most cases, teams are largely dependent on the star players. In fact, how well the star players play often determines whether the team will win or not. While there are star players, there are also those who ride the bench who do not normally play in games. Nevertheless, when the championship is won, those who ride the bench have the same excitement as the star players because they receive the same reward, although they made no contributions to the victory.

In life, we face many battles in which we feel the need to make a contribution. *I need to do this. I need to do that. I need to say this. I need to handle it this way.* And on and on. When it comes to battles in life, we have to remember we have a Star Player and the victories of life are totally dependent on how *He* plays — not us. It is important that we *ride the bench* and not attempt to do what only the Star Player can do. Allow God to fight your battles. Sit back and cheer Him on as He handles those situations you cannot handle alone. "Go, God, go!" Even if you make no contribution, when the battle is won, you will receive the reward with the same excitement when all you did was ride the bench and trust in your Star Player.

You've Grown Up

"Therefore if anyone is in Christ, the new creation has come: The old has gone, the new is here!"

— *II Corinthians 5:17 (NIV)*

Around May of each year, I receive invitations to attend the graduations of family members, friends and youth from the church. Included in some invitations are the graduate's senior photos. The photos are taken in the senior year of high school to be given to family and friends as a memoir of a person's physical appearance as graduation nears. On one occasion, I received an invitation from a cousin I have not seen in years and when I looked at the picture, I said, "Boy, he has really grown up!" Immediately I began to reflect back to my own high school graduation, so I began to flip through my senior yearbook. When I came across my picture and saw the baby face in the photo compared to the black and gray beard I have today, I concluded, "Boy, you have really grown up!"

There are many situations and ways of life that Christians come from. We dare not detail the dealings of the past. Certainly, no one is more aware of your past than you are. Nevertheless, when you think about who you once were compared to who you are now, you can now say, "Boy, have I grown up!" "I used to do this, but now I do this," and "I used to say this, but now I do this," are some of the testimonies many of us have. All of us are an ex-something. There is nothing wrong with being an ex-something as long as your ex-something is still an ex. Staying in touch with where God brought you from is paramount, so that when you flip through the yearbook of the past, God and you both can say, "(your name), you have really grown up!"

Don't Kiss Me

"… For all have sinned and fall short of the glory of God, and are justified freely by his grace through the redemption that came by Christ Jesus. God presented Christ as a sacrifice of atonement, through the shedding of his blood – to be received by faith. He did this to demonstrate his righteousness, because in his forbearance he had left the sins committed beforehand unpunished — he did it to demonstrate his righteousness at the present time, so as to be just and the one who justifies those who have faith in Jesus."

— Romans 3:23-26 (NIV)

At Christmas time, many people hang mistletoe at the entrance of their homes. It is said that every time someone is found to be under the mistletoe, that person is to be kissed. I have seen some people hold the mistletoe above their own head in order to be kissed by someone else. People who do not like the mistletoe concept will pass under the mistletoe very quickly and when someone tries to kiss them they say, "I have already passed the mistletoe, so don't try to kiss me!" For some, the concept of the mistletoe is fun and exciting at Christmas, but not so fun in the Christian life.

All of us have done and said some things that we are not proud of. However, it is also important that we not stand under Satan's mistletoe of guilt. When we are under Satan's mistletoe, he kisses us with thoughts of unworthiness, depression, lack of faith, and other harmful kisses. For some of us, Satan's "lipstick" has been on some of us for weeks, months, or possibly years! With the Christmas mistletoe, once you have passed under it, the opportunity for someone to kiss you has been forfeited, unless you deem otherwise. Each time Satan attempts to hang his mistletoe of guilt over your head, you need to decree and declare, "Satan, I have passed that, God has forgiven me, therefore, don't even try to kiss me!"

Whenever, Wherever, Whoever

"And do not grieve the Holy Spirit of God, with whom you were sealed for the day of redemption."

— *Ephesians 4:30 (NIV)*

Have you felt the spirit of God move upon you to the point where you just wanted to run around your house or church in praise and thanksgiving to God? You felt the urge to shout, "Thank you Jesus!" to the top of your lungs. You felt the tears of joy welling up in your eyes and you wanted to cry? I have seen people literally make themselves sick trying to hold these things in. Here is the question: Did you give in to the urge to praise and worship? If not, why?

There are many times in and outside of the church when the spirit of God moves upon us — in the car, home, church, and at work. We can feel the desire to praise and worship God, but push it away because of where we are, whom we are around, and/or what people may think. To my knowledge, the Bible does not note a place where it is inappropriate to praise and worship God. There are many ways we can praise and worship God regardless of the time and location. Of course, we may not be able to run and shout at the top of our lungs in the office or classroom, but a whisper of praise is always appropriate. When the Spirit moves upon you, do not focus on your surroundings, but direct your attention towards God and give Him the worship and praise He deserves whenever, wherever, and regardless of whoever is around!

Get Out of Debt

"If your brother sins, go and point out their fault, just between the two of you. If they listen to you, you have won them over."

— *Matthew 18:15 (NIV)*

There are many people who are in credit card debt and to them it seems virtually impossible to be debt free. Interest rates on some credit cards are very high, and some people expect to get out of debt paying the minimum payment. Paying minimum payments is paying just enough to avoid late fees, receive letters, or maintain a decent credit rating. The best way to manage a credit card is that when it is charged, it is paid.

Neo-Soul artist, India Arie, penned a song that includes the lyrics, "No one has the power to hurt you like your kin," and "No one has the power to hurt you like your friends." Certainly, many of us can relate to being hurt by family or friends. Often times, when someone hurts us, we push it to the back of our minds and try to move forward — that is a minimum payment. Before long, pushing it to the back of the mind, or ignoring it adds interest called resentment, revenge, and other things. It is understood that people are able to move forward doing this, but the debt (hurt) still remains and needs to be dealt with. If you are holding on to the hurt someone has caused you, deal with it before the interest accrues.

The Enemy Has a Hall Pass

"Moreover, demons came out of many people, shouting, 'You are the Son of God!' But he rebuked them and would not allow them to speak, because they knew he was the Messiah.

—Luke 4:41 (NIV)

Reflecting on the days of grade school, I remember that every teacher had what was commonly called, a hall pass. Each teacher's hall pass may have been a different color or size, but each one had the same significance. Whenever a student wanted to go to the restroom, get a drink of water, run an errand for the teacher, or anything else that required them to be in the hallway, he would need a hall pass. When the principal or others saw the hall pass, they then knew that the teacher had given that student permission to be outside of the classroom.

Some of us wonder why we experience the things we experience. It seems that Satan is relentless in his attacks. He is attacking your family, job, children, health, and other areas. If you are not careful, you can reach a point where you feel like giving up because the enemy's attacks seem to be too much to handle. Know today that Satan must obtain a hall pass (permission) from The Teacher to attack your life. As in grade school, the one with the hall pass cannot stay in halls for an extended period of time. Demons cannot even speak without God's permission! Therefore, when you see the enemy's attacks on your life, know God has given him limited permission and He will not put more on you than you can bear.

It Happens in the Dark

"...When his lamp shone on my head and by his light I walked through darkness!"

—*Job 29:3 (NIV)*

"Even though I walk through the valley, I will fear no evil, for you are with me; your rod and your staff, they comfort me."

—*Psalm 23:4 (NIV)*

During the photo developing process, it is important that the area be dark so the photos can be developed without flaws. If the photos are exposed to light, there is a good chance that they will be ruined. In college, I worked as a photo lab technician responsible for developing quality pictures. As the pictures are developed in the dark, the machine automatically adjusts the color that is needed. Sometimes I would need to change the color a little by touching a button or two, however, most of the time the adjustments were automatic.

Have you ever been in the darkroom of life? You have no idea why things are happening the way they are. You do not understand why you feel a certain way. You do not know how it is going to be accomplished. You must know that it is while in the dark that God develops the character and trust you need to be the quality Christian He wants you to be. Of course, you don't know the specifics of the situation and you often think about them. However, know that you don't have to do a thing because God automatically makes the needed adjustments while you are in the darkroom. You may be in the darkroom of life right now, and although you have no clue how tomorrow will turn out, please know you are being "developed!"

It is In Your Mouth

"The tongue has the power of life and death, and those who love it will eat its fruit."

— Proverbs 18:21 (NIV)

COPS used to be one of my favorite shows. On one episode, the officer stopped this guy and he smelled alcohol on his breath. The officer suspected that the man was under the influence simply because of what was coming out of his mouth. The officer asked the man if he would be willing to take a Breathalyzer test. The officer explained that when the man blew into a tube, a computer would provide a reading using the man's breath to determine the amount of alcohol in his system. In short, the Breathalyzer test simply reads what comes out of the mouth to determine what's on the inside.

Brothers and sisters, people should be able to determine who or what we are influenced by simply on the basis of what comes out of our mouths. What if God were to give us a Breathalyzer test to read His level of influence by what comes out of our mouths? *What would the reading be?* My brother, my sister, speak life to whatever you are facing. Speak life over yourself. Furthermore, be sure not to be one who speaks about faith but not one who speaks in faith. People around us should not only see your faith, but hear your faith, ultimately arriving at the conclusion that Jesus resides deeply within. It's in your mouth!

Yes, You Can

"I can do all this through Him who gives me strength."

—Philippians 4:13 (NIV)

In our youth ministry, there are two words that are simply illegal to say if used in the wrong context: "I can't." If someone is asked to read or complete a ministry task, it is illegal to say, "I can't." If someone is asked to come out of the comfort zone to build his or her faith, the youth often want to say, "I can't." However, knowing these words are frowned upon in the ministry, it causes the youth to move beyond their comfort zones and discover they can do more than they imagine - through Christ Jesus.

Though rudimentary, this is a concept many adults can adopt. If we think about it, many of us say, "I can't," to things simply because it is not within our comfort zone. I have never taught Sunday School, so I can't. I have never been on the program to speak, so I can't. I have never evangelized, so I can't. They've upset me and I am supposed to forgive, but I can't. This list can go on forever! However, if we live our lives according to today's Scripture, we will be able to move beyond our comfort zone and allow God to show us that He can and will do through us more than we ever imagined. At this point in life, you may be saying, "I can't" to something, but it is time for you to move beyond "I can't" to "I can." Through Christ, you can do all things!

There is More in You

"Let us not become weary in doing good, for at the proper time we will reap a harvest if we do not give up."

— Galatians 6:9 (NIV)

When I would bathe my toddler son, one of his favorite things to do would be to wring out the towel. It was always amusing to watch him grimace as he used all of his strength to ensure he removed all of the water from the towel. After he would exert all of his effort, he would hand the towel to me as if to say, "I have gotten it all out." When I would get the towel, I would wring it out and he was amazed to see so much water come from it. On one occasion, he said "I thought I got it all out." I replied, "I know you did, but your father is able to get more out of it than you can."

As we conclude this devotional book, there are, or will be, times when you feel you have taken all you can take. You will feel that you cannot bear any more. There are moments when you will say, "I don't know what else to do, I have done all I know to do." The truth is, that may very well be the case, however, something else is also true — God can get more out that you can. As you conclude this book and move on to something else, just know God has more in you. While you are doing whatever you can to achieve whatever it is you are trying to do, know your Father can get more out of you. In the words of one of my pastor mentors, Laurence Hudson, do what you can and trust God to do what you can't.

Author Bio

Pastor Timothy Jackson, Jr. is the proud husband of Ashiqua Jackson, father of three beautiful children, Ava MaeRee, and twins, Timothy III and Avery Juliette. He serves as the Senior Pastor of Hope Fellowship Church in Memphis, Tennessee.

Pastor Jackson is a 1995 graduate of Whitehaven High School. He went on to attend the University of Tennessee at Chattanooga, where he earned a Bachelor of Science in Environmental Science with an emphasis in Biology and became a proud member of Kappa Alpha Psi Fraternity. For the fraternity, he served as Kappa League Chairman and later served as President of the chapter.

Pastor Jackson culminated his undergraduate college career by being voted the first and only African-American Mr. University of Tennessee at Chattanooga. In 2012, he graduated with a Master of Christian Studies degree from Union University. Three weeks after his graduation, he entered the Doctor of Ministry program at United Theological Seminary in Dayton, Ohio and graduated May 2015.

Jackson accepted his call to ministry September 4, 2000. Over the years, he has appeared on television, magazines, and radio along with opportunities to speak at many churches and conferences. In the early 2000s, Pastor Jackson authored an online devotional ministry entitled "Talk to Me God" that blessed the lives of thousands of people around the globe, including Australia, France and Hong Kong. Entries from the devotional ministry were published in Malaysia and the United Kingdom. Considered to be gifted with the ability to craft sermon illustrations, pastors from around the country seek him for sermon illustrations and advice in producing them. Several sermon illustrations have been published on the website of *The African American Lectionary*, providing opportunity for ministers and pastors throughout the world to tap into his gift. In addition to ministry, Pastor Jackson works as a Senior Environmental Specialist at FedEx Express Corporation, where he serves as a liaison between FedEx and environmental agencies, training employees and monitoring environmental compliance for more than 100 FedEx Express facilities throughout the United States.

Because of his wide range of pastoral and corporate experiences, he has been sought after to provide leadership advice in both corporate and church arenas. He is particularly passionate about new leaders, young ministers, and new pastors. Pastor Jackson equips them with knowledge when entering a new leadership role, and helps them avoid many of the pitfalls encountered by new leaders.

Pastor Jackson is committed to playing an instrumental role in the building of people so that they may build up their families, communities, organizations, and churches. He strives to promote excellence spiritually, socially, and academically to people of all ages. It is his prayer that God will use him to impact the lives of people in the church, city, and nation.

Notes

Notes

Notes

Notes

Notes

Notes

Notes

Notes

Notes

Notes

**If you liked this book,
I invite you to leave a positive review
on Amazon.com.**

Search for:
"Talk To Me God" by Dr. Timothy Jackson Jr.